SHADOWS OF TIME

BRYAN PAUL LAI

INDIA • SINGAPORE • MALAYSIA

Contents

Synopsis of The Story

Stories of Sabah`s Struggle and Resilience

SABAH THE LAND BELOW THE WIND

THE PANAROMIC AND ALLURING VIEW OF MOUNT KINABALU
IN SABAH

Set against the backdrop of Sabah, the land below the wind stood still, eighty momentous years, chronicling a journey through the triumphs and tribulations of humanity. The story captures an era of transformation, from the scars of war and colonialism to the dawn of modern Malaysia and the unprecedented challenges of a global pandemic.

The narrative begins with echoes of the past—a time when tribal conflicts and ravenousness shaped the land. These seeds of discord persist, emerging periodically to fuel inequality, war, and societal strife. As Sabah evolves, its people face new trials, navigating through World War II, the tumultuous years of colonial rule, the formation of Malaysia, and the political tensions of the Indonesia–Malaysia Confrontation. Each event leaves an indelible mark on the region and its people, shaping their identity and resilience.The story then shifts to the rise of political adventurism. Leaders, often emerging from humble beginnings, succumb to the temptations of power and wealth. The innocent, hopeful youth are left disillusioned, caught in a cycle of broken promises and systemic exploitation. Amidst this, the land struggles to reconcile its tribal roots with the pressures of modernization and globalization. In 2020, an unanticipated crisis strikes—a virus unlike anything the world has known.

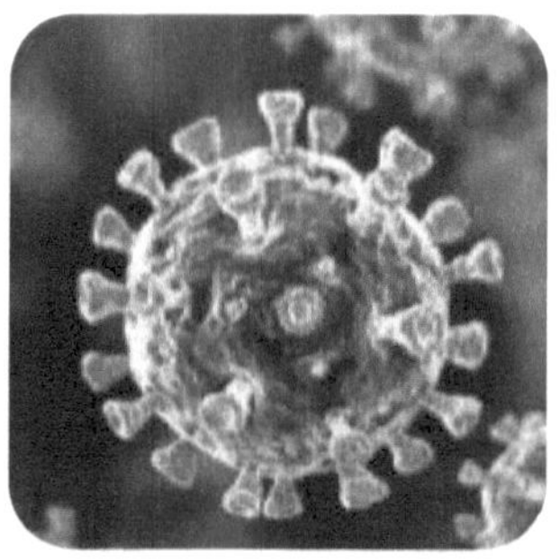

COVID 19

COVID-19 upends the fabric of human society overnight, spreading chaos and fear. The pandemic reveals both the best and worst of humanity. Scientists and experts rally to confront the crisis, working tirelessly to uncover the virus's origins and develop solutions. Yet, hidden beneath the surface is a shadowy narrative of secrecy and suspicion. Was the virus a natural calamity or a product of human greed and ambition? The global blame game ensues, deepening divisions and leaving questions unanswered.

As the pandemic rages, the story examines the fragility of human systems and the resilience of the human spirit. From bustling cities to remote villages, no one is spared. Yet, even amidst the devastation, glimmers of hope emerge. Humanity's ingenuity and determination come to the forefront, offering a vision of how the world might adapt and rebuild.

Blending historical events with fictionalized elements, the land below the wind stood still is a profound meditation on the human condition. It explores themes of greed, resilience, and the relentless pursuit of progress. At its heart, the story poses an enduring question: will the advances of this new era lead humanity to a brighter future, or will they sow the seeds of its downfall?

A poignant reflection on Sabah's history and the shared struggles of humanity, the book serves as a reminder of life's unpredictability—akin to a storm at sea. It Honors the resilience of a land and its people, while urging readers to reflect on their place in an ever-changing world.

First Episode

Kota Kinabalu city

Prior to the covid 19 contagion Kota Kinabalu: A Vibrant City, the capital city of Sabah, stands as a vibrant tapestry of humanity, where people of diverse racial and cultural backgrounds have coexisted harmoniously since the Austronesian era. This bustling city, nestled against the backdrop of the majestic Mount Kinabalu—the highest peak in Southeast Asia—is a hub for adventurers and seekers of natural beauty. The mountain, often referred to as the "Land Below the Wind," is a magnet for both local and international tourists, offering a glimpse of Sabah's unparalleled charm among the clouds Just beyond the city lies Penampang, a hamlet that was once Sabah's breadbasket, with sprawling paddy fields stretching as far as the eye could see. The sight of buffaloes labouring in these fields is now a memory of the past, as urbanization gradually reshapes the landscape. However, the timeless beauty of its rivers and hills preserves the essence of an untouched countryside. Daily Activities and Community Engagement the year 2020 began as another ordinary year for Sabah's communities, filled with daily toil and vibrant social activities.

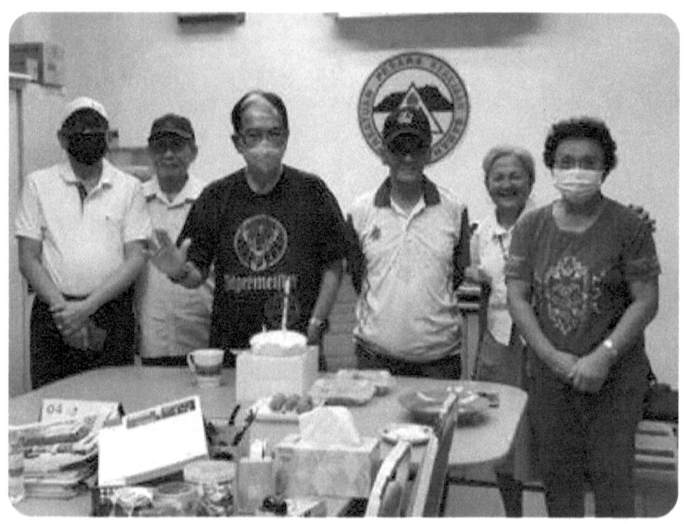

Datuk Wilfred Lingham and his duly elected committee

The Sabah Government Pensioners Association, led by Datuk Wilfred Lingham, worked tirelessly to ensure that its programs for the year would benefit members across the state's 22 districts. Encik Hamid Harun, the Secretary General, dedicated significant time to coordinating these initiatives, which included health seminars and outreach programs aimed at unregistered pensioners. These efforts were supported by the Sabah Council of Social Services (MPMS), which allocated resources for activities benefiting the aging population. Events like the "Pra Pesara Seminar," with guest speakers such as Tan Sri Simon Sipaun, former Sabah State Secretary during the Colony days brought valuable insights to attendees.

Tan Sri Simon Sipaun addressing the pensioners

Whilst Hanid the secretary general stood watch

Meanwhile, Kota Kinabalu's international airport remained a bustling gateway, welcoming tourists who fuelled the local economy. Hotels were fully booked, shops thrived, and schools operated on schedule, creating a sense of normalcy.

MPMS programme continued to function normally prior to the shadows of covid 19

From left Bryan Paul Lai. Stella Wan Hamid Harun and Joseph Wong executive committee of PPKS

The Kota Kinabalu Municipal Council Organised a one-day seminar for senior citizen from left Datuk Wilfred Lingham Datuk Nordin Siman and official from Kota Kinabalu Municipal Council

The participants attending the seminar at the council premises at Kingfisher district

The Onset of the COVID-19 Pandemic By early 2020, the global community was becoming increasingly aware of the impending threat posed by the COVID-19 pandemic. In Sabah, life carried on with cautious optimism as the government closely monitored developments. Preparations for significant cultural events—such as the Muslim community's Puasa Month in April and the Kadazan-Dusun grand harvest festival in May—proceeded as planned.

Activities continued to function before covid19 by the ministry off Health.

However, the looming shadow of the pandemic was undeniable. International borders began to close, and countries implemented strict measures to curb the virus's spread. The Malaysian federal government, anticipating the inevitable, prepared to implement a paradigm shift that would alter the nation's trajectory. Resilience in the Face of adversity. Despite the challenges, the local community in Sabah demonstrated remarkable resilience. Healthcare professionals worked tirelessly to implement the government's well-prepared algorithms, ensuring that medical facilities were equipped to handle the crisis. Community organizations adapted quickly, shifting their focus to support vulnerable populations during the lockdown. The government's proactive measures, though difficult, were instrumental in minimizing the impact of the pandemic.

The COVID-19 pandemic significantly affected the people of Sabah, Malaysia, causing widespread social, economic, and health challenges. Here's a summary of its impact: Health and Healthcare System: Sabah's healthcare system, already under strain, faced overwhelming pressure as COVID-19 cases surged. Hospitals in major cities like Kota Kinabalu, Sandakan and Tawau were stretched, with limited capacity to handle the growing number of patients. Vaccination campaigns were launched, but rural areas faced challenges in accessing vaccines due to logistical barriers. Despite these hurdles, Sabah achieved significant vaccination coverage by mid- Economic Impact: Tourism and Hospitality: Sabah's tourism-dependent economy suffered a major blow, with the closure of international borders and lockdowns leading to a sharp decline in visitors. Many workers in tourism, hospitality, and transportation lost their jobs or faced reduced income. Agriculture and Fisheries: Sabah's agriculture sector, particularly palm oil and fisheries, faced disruptions in supply chains. Local and international demand for agricultural products decreased, affecting the livelihoods of farmers and fishermen. Job Losses and Financial Strain: Many individuals in the informal sector, such as small traders and daily-wage workers, faced economic hardship. While the government provided some financial aid, it was often insufficient, especially for those without access to support programs. Social and Cultural Impact: Social Isolation and Mental Health: The pandemic caused significant social isolation due to lockdowns and movement restrictions. Mental health issues, such as anxiety and depression, increased, especially among vulnerable groups like the elderly and those with pre-existing conditions. Education Disruptions: Schools in Sabah switched to online learning, which posed challenges due to limited internet access and digital infrastructure in rural areas. Many students struggled to keep up with their studies. Religious and Cultural Gatherings: Religious practices and cultural activities were disrupted, with mosques, churches, and temples often closed or operating under strict guidelines. Festivals and communal gatherings were limited or cancelled, affecting community life. Community Response and Solidarity: Volunteer and Community Support: In response to the pandemic, various community groups and NGOs in Sabah mobilized to provide food, medical supplies, and support to those in need. Local residents came together to assist vulnerable groups. Government Measures: The state government introduced relief packages and financial assistance to mitigate the impact of the pandemic. However, the reach and effectiveness of these measures varied, with some communities experiencing delays or insufficient support. Long-Term Effects: The long-term effects of COVID-19 in Sabah include continued economic recovery challenges, particularly in tourism and small businesses. There are also concerns about the lasting mental health impact on the population, especially among those who have lost jobs or loved ones. In conclusion, while Sabah faced significant challenges due to COVID-19, the pandemic also highlighted the resilience and solidarity of its people. The road to recovery is ongoing, with efforts focused on rebuilding the economy, addressing mental health concerns, and ensuring equitable access to healthcare and vaccines. Feeling of despair as covid 19 spread Many unfortunate ones unable to get immediate help dropped dead like flies on the streets, pathways, shop lots, and open spaces. Mortuaries were overwhelmed - churning out as many bags as fast as they could to cope with the hundreds of bodies coming in by the minutes. A dreadful emotional sight to behold as hundreds of coffins laid out in rows awaiting burial or cremation. Gravediggers worked throughout, under the unrelenting sun to bury the dead.

Dead bodies waiting for cremation

Cremation centres were at overawed with full capacity, to dispose the deceased. A living nightmare to behold. Looking back at the scenario, compelled me to recount just how this virus and its contagion struck the entire world like a bolt of lightning, devoid of clemency and sympathy, and how it has impacted everyone. Is COVID-19 an antidote for planet earth? A view that some religious bodies and soothsayers subscribe too. Such a view may be farfetched but there is some report by the United Nation that earth is in a red zone and action must be taken to solve the problem before it becomes irreversible. For the past two hundred years, humans, driven by greed, have assaulted the earth with their quest to enrich themselves beyond their need. And the earth fought back with a vengeance. It is up to us to pay it back and to salvage the destruction caused by our kind. The urgent need to speed up the world's environment has to start now. The world is our only home akin to Noah's Ark. We must work together to save our home before it is too late. The emergence of refugees due to circumstances brought by our kinds such as war, destruction, genocide and human ravenousness need to be heard before the voices of discontent erupt. The lives of millions are forever changed due to this pandemic. People from around the globe are still trying to make sense of it all. Families torn apart by geography and death are now coming terms to with the situation and are trying their best to move forward in a new frontier. The world of today is again back to its historical greed to claim the worlds resources by the smart alike of the world The impact of COVID-19 has profoundly disrupted the Sabah community, exacerbating an already challenging situation. As the pandemic's severity escalated globally, the Ministry of Health was compelled to declare a lockdown effective from midnight on September 28th. Hospitals in Tawau swiftly erected multiple temporary shelters to accommodate the surge of patients. After several months, Malaysia's infection rate began to stabilize. As of September 28, 2020, reports surfaced via WhatsApp that four districts on Sabah's east coast were designated as red zones, prompting military and police to enforce strict movement restrictions. The re-introduction of the Movement Control Order (MCO) resulted in school closures due to alarming infection rates in October. Penampang district was subsequently placed under a severe maximum lockdown for several months. When the MCO eventually eased, there was a brief sense of relief as daily routines resumed for schools, associations, and workers. However, this respite was short-lived and illusory, as the global surge in COVID-19 cases heralded the onset of second waves. Borders remained tightly sealed, urging everyone to stay indoors. Beyond the east coast, other towns also faced repercussions, plunging businesses that had begun to recover back into uncertainty The temporary calm shattered as infections surged in towns like Tawau, Lahad Datu, Semporna, and Kunak. Numerous clusters emerged, spreading rapidly throughout every corner of the state. This unfolding crisis marked a historical moment where a disease's reach extended deep into communities worldwide, presenting unprecedented. Challenges for governments and citizens alike Amid the escalating COVID-19 situation across Malaysia, the government implemented stringent Standard Operating Procedures (SOPs) in several districts, notably

Tawau, Semporna, Lahad Datu, Kunak, Kota Kinabalu, Penampang, and Inanam. These measures were enforced from October 3rd to 18th, depending on the severity of outbreaks in each area. Subsequently, a Movement Control Order (MCO) was reintroduced, effective from midnight on October 7th until October 18t... As a pensioner and concerned family member, we felt a growing sense of unease as the virus continued to spread unabated, affecting numerous lives. Sabah once again found itself under strict MCO measures, necessitating quarantine and heightened precautions to manage the increasing healthcare demand, the Health Ministry swiftly erected temporary shelters and utilized sports complexes to accommodate overflow medical facilities. Contractors were mobilized urgently to execute these plans. Additionally, the Health Ministry explored collaborations with private hospitals, preparing for a potential surge in cases to ensure readiness at critical levels Episode 4 Effect of Covid 19 The Populace's dilemma

The Medical Fraternity such as Fatimah and other nurses, has always believed in the power of compassion and perseverance. They work tirelessly at hospital in Sabah, a Malaysian state known for its lush rainforests and diverse cultures. The health service department in Sabah has come a long way, boasting several well-equipped hospitals in all major towns. Every small district has its own operational clinics, providing basic healthcare to the local communities. Over the years, the healthcare system has seen significant improvements, including the addition of a flying doctor service to reach the remote, far-flung villages scattered across the state. However, the ever-increasing influx of illegal migrants and the rapid population growth have turned the quest for quality healthcare into a daunting challenge. The waiting time for patients has stretched longer, and complaints have become a regular background hum in the hospital corridors. The administration is acutely aware of these constraints and is constantly striving to find amicable solutions. Public hospitals cater to the ordinary populace of Malaysia, offering essential services to all who need them. In addition, private hospitals and clinics stand ready to serve those who can afford their fees. Despite the addition of more doctors to bridge the gap, the supply still struggles to keep pace with the burgeoning population. Fatimah's a typical nurse in a government hospital begins before dawn. She navigates the bustling hospital corridors with practiced ease, her presence a guiding light of calm amidst the chaos. Her patients come from all walks of life – from local villagers to city dwellers, from expectant mothers to the elderly. Each one has a story, and Fatimah listens, her gentle demeanor providing comfort and reassurance. One of her regular patients, an elderly man named Pak Kassim, often shares tales of his youth in the serene hills of Ranau. Fatimah always makes time to listen, knowing that for Pak Kassim, these conversations are a lifeline. She knows the importance of human connection in the healing process. One rainy afternoon, a young boy from a distant village arrives, bringing his sickly grandfather. The flying doctor service under the care of health worker Joseph Jominol had brought them to the hospital, a salvation for those in remote areas. The nurses spring into action, Fatimah who was on duty on that day administers care with a steady hand and a compassionate heart, providing not just medical treatment, but also a sense of hope. Despite the challenges, Fatimah remains undeterred

She is driven by a deep sense of duty and an unwavering commitment to her patients. The long hours, the endless stream of patients, and the occasional disgruntled complaint all fade away when she sees a patient smile, when she hears a heartfelt 'thank you,' or when she witnesses the spark of recovery in a patient's eyes. Every evening, as Fatimah leaves the hospital, she feels a sense of fulfillment. She knows that the road ahead is fraught with challenges, but she also knows that each day she makes a difference, one patient at a time. The health service in Sabah continues to evolve, and with dedicated professionals like doctors and nurses, there is always hope for a brighter, healthier future. Nurses and healthcare workers in Sabah are locally trained by several institutions, striving to fill the critical gaps in the nursing fraternity. This is the story of Mariam, a young graduate nurse who had just qualified and secured a job at a government hospital during the harrowing days of the COVID-19 pandemic.

When Mariam a novice who had just qualified from the nursing school received the job offer, her heart soared with enthusiasm and high spirits. Despite a twinge of disappointment at not being assigned to her far-flung village, she felt a deep sense of pride. Securing a government job had been her lifelong dream—not just for herself, but to support her aging parents. As a kampong girl, leaving her family home was the hardest choice she ever had to make. The moment she arrived in Kota Kinabalu, the bustling capital of Sabah, Mariam was greeted by her mother's sister. Her aunt welcomed her warmly and offered her a temporary place to stay, a comforting oasis in an unfamiliar city. The next day, Mariam reported for duty at the hospital, stepping into a whirlwind of activity and urgency. The hospital was a hive of chaotic energy, a stark contrast to the serene village life she had known. As she walked through the corridors, she felt the weight of the pandemic's impact. The air was thick with a sense of urgency and tension, mingling with the antiseptic smell of the hospital. Nurses and doctors moved with purpose; their faces marked by fatigue yet driven by a shared mission. Assigned to a ward, Mariam stood by, awaiting her first task. Patients overflowed the beds, their faces masked with both cloth and fear. The relentless beeping of monitors and the hushed, urgent voices of medical staff created a cacophony of stress and determination. Despite the overwhelming situation, Mariam felt a surge of determination. She recalled the rigorous training she had undergone, the late nights of studying, and the countless hours of practical work. Now, it was time to put all of that into practice. She was ready to face the challenge head-on, to bring her knowledge and compassion to the front lines. Her first task was assisting a senior nurse with the care of a critically ill patient. As she donned her protective gear, her hands shook slightly, but her resolve remained firm. She followed instructions meticulously, her movements a blend of caution and confidence. The senior nurse, sensing Mariams determination, offered a reassuring nod, a silent acknowledgment of her capability. Days turned into weeks, and Mariam quickly adapted to the relentless pace. She became a familiar face in the ward, her presence a blend of youthful energy and unwavering dedication. Her patients, many isolated from their families, found solace in her kindness and gentle care. Despite the masks, her eyes conveyed warmth and empathy, bridging the gap created by the virus. Every evening, as Mariam returned to her aunt's home, she felt a profound sense of accomplishment. The challenges were immense, the hours long, but she knew she was making a difference. She was not just a nurse; she was a beacon of hope in the darkest of times, embodying the spirit of resilience and compassion that Sabah needed. Mariams journey had only just begun, but she knew that with each patient she helped, she was contributing to a legacy of care and dedication that would outlast the pandemic. And in her heart, she carried the dreams and hopes of her village, knowing that one day, she would return, stronger and more capable, to serve her community. Three months had passed, and Mariam had proven herself to be a capable and dedicated nurse. She had swiftly acquired the necessary skills and the intricate algorithms required to perform her duties with precision. Her confidence grew with each passing day as she navigated the complexities of patient care. Mariam, though slightly apprehensive, remained calm. She remembered her training and the experiences of the past three months. As she donned her protective gear and prepared to enter the ward, she felt a surge of determination. This was the moment she had been trained for, the moment where her skills and dedication would be put to the ultimate test. The ward, now designated for COVID-19 patients, was a scene of intense activity. Medical staff moved with purpose, setting up isolation areas and preparing equipment. Mariam's heart pounded as she took in the gravity of the situation, but she steadied herself. She approached her first COVID-19 patient, a middle-aged man struggling to breathe, with a calm and composed demeanour. She meticulously followed the new protocols, ensuring every step was taken to protect both the patient and herself. The patient's laboured breathing and the rhythmic beeping of the monitors filled the room, creating a sombre symphony of the pandemic's reality. Mariam's hands moved with precision, her eyes reflecting a mixture of empathy and resolve Mariam found herself working longer hours, her days blending into nights. Yet, despite the exhaustion, she remained steadfast. Her colleagues, inspired by her unwavering dedication, rallied together, forming a united front against the virus. Each evening, as Mariam returned to her aunt's home, she felt a profound mix of exhaustion and fulfillment. The road ahead was uncertain, and the challenges were immense, but she knew she was part of something greater. She was not just fighting a virus; she was upholding the spirit of care and resilience that defined Sabah's healthcare workers. Mariam's journey was far from over. She knew that her role was crucial, that her hands, though small, carried the weight of hope and healing. And with every act of care, she fortified her commitment to the people of Sabah, ready to face whatever lay ahead. By the end of each gruelling day, Mariam was exhausted to the core.

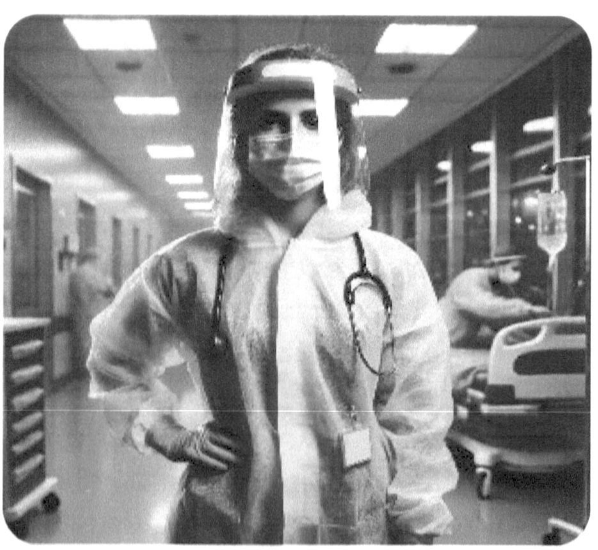

Used of protective attire is mandatory

Clad in full protective attire, she and her colleagues took moments to ease their physical and spiritual trauma, finding brief solace in shared glances and whispered words of encouragement., Mariam and her fellow nurses managed to find a sliver of solace in their isolated dormitory. The experience was relentless, testing their endurance and spirit. While they provided care to the infected, their own safety was paramount. The psychological toll was immense, and even the hardest souls among them were brought to tears as they watched patients being wrapped for burial without their families present.

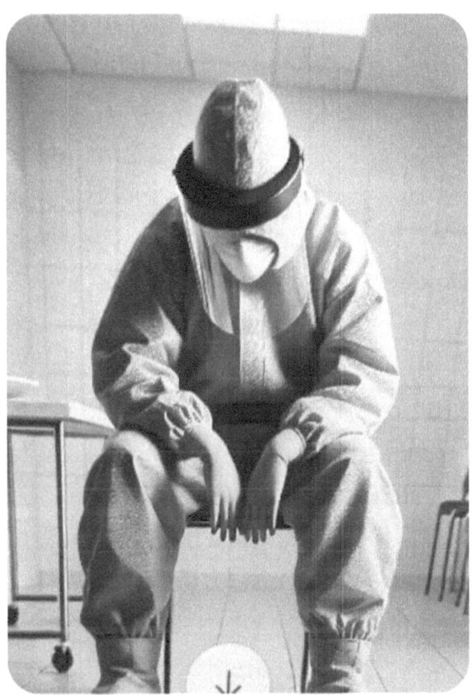

Exhausted health worker

Mariam and the other nurses could not stop tears from flowing as they witnessed the death surrounding the room. The heart-wrenching scenes played out repeatedly, a grim reminder of the pandemic's brutal reality. As the days blurred together, Mariam's resilience was tested to its limits. The weight of each loss, each life that slipped away, bore down on her heart. She found herself comforting not only her patients but also her colleagues, their shared grief forging an unbreakable bond. Together, they navigated the uncharted waters of the pandemic, their collective strength a ray of hope amidst the darkness. Despite the overwhelming fatigue and emotional strain, their role was critical, an instruments of care and compassion. Every act of kindness, every moment of connection, reinforced her commitment to her patients and her community. The pandemic had cast a long shadow, but within it, Mariam and her fellow healthcare workers stood as pillars of light, determined to face whatever challenges lay ahead. Mariam occasionally had nightmares, haunted by the tragedies she had witnessed. The daily chores and duties took a profound toll on the nurses, leaving an indelible impact on their physical and spiritual well-being. Mariam found herself in an unexpected and surreal scenario, struggling to keep up with the hectic demands of her duties. Despite the discomfort and the relentless pace, Mariam pushed forward. The sight of patients, eyes filled with fear and desperation, fuelled her extermination. She moved from bed to bed, administering care with a steady hand, her eyes offering reassurance even when words failed. The hospital, once a place of healing, now felt like a battleground. The constant influx of patients created an atmosphere of urgency and despair. Mariam and her colleagues worked tirelessly; their faces etched with fatigue but their spirits unyielding. They found brief moments of respite in each other's company, sharing quiet words of support amidst the chaos. occasionally took a moment to step outside, inhaling the cool night air in an attempt to clear her mind. The stars above seemed distant and indifferent, a stark contrast to the turmoil within the hospital walls. She thought of her family, her village, and the life she had left behind. Each memory served as a reminder of why she had chosen this path. In the dimly lit corridors, were filled with restless sleep and vivid dreams, the faces of the deceased and the ailing flashing through her mind. She knew that the psychological scars of this period would linger long after the pandemic had passed. Yet, despite the nightmares, she woke each day with renewed resolve, ready to face the unrelenting tide of patients. The nurses' camaraderie became a lifeline. They shared stories, laughter, and tears, finding strength in their unity. They leaned on each other, their collective resolve a bulwark against the encroaching despair, shared experiences forging bonds that would endure far beyond the crisis. She knew that the path ahead was fraught with challenges, but she was ready to meet them head-on. With every patient she helped, she fortified her commitment to her calling, embodying the resilience and spirit that defined Sabah's healthcare workers. Meanwhile, Johana - a dedicated nurse in Kota Kinabalu, working in a private clinic had initially underestimated the gravity of the pandemic. As news of the virus spread, her routine at the clinic took a dramatic turn. The sudden collapse of a patient outside the clinic underscored the virus's proximity, plunging her into a state of vigilance. Isolating herself from her family became an immediate priority, driven by her concern for her vulnerable household members. Her days were marked by anxious waits for test results, the weight of responsibility heavy on her shoulders. Meanwhile, Datuk Wilfred Lingham President of PPKS, viewed the lockdown as a mere inconvenience in his well-established routine. Stocked with provisions and protected by vaccination, he navigated the restrictions with resilience born of past challenges. For him, the pandemic was a temporary disruption, As the days turned into months, the people of Sabah adjusted to the new normal, finding innovative ways to stay connected and support one another. Virtual gatherings replaced physical events, and the spirit of unity remained unbroken. While the pandemic disrupted lives and livelihoods, it also highlighted the strength and resilience of Sabah's diverse communities. Together, they navigated the storm, emerging with renewed determination to rebuild and thrive in the post-pandemic era. The Movement Control Order (MCO)On 18 March 2020, Malaysia's Movement Control Order (MCO) was imposed nationwide. This measure incorporated strict restrictions on movement, assembly, and international travel. Businesses, industries, government offices, and educational institutions were mandated to close, with exemptions granted only for critical services. For the people of Sabah, the MCO marked the beginning of an unprecedented chapter. Families were confined to their homes, facing weeks and eventually months of uncertainty. The vibrant cityscapes and bustling streets of Kota Kinabalu fell silent, as the virus spread rapidly, leaving no aspect of life untouched. As the months goes by the medical department flying doctor service, to remote villages had been intensified. The project became a lifeline for many, providing vaccinations, prenatal care, and health education to communities that had been overlooked for decades. These moments, however brief, provided a lifeline to those teetering on the edge of despair. The camaraderie among the nurses grew stronger, their shared stories forming an unspoken pact to see each other through the crisis. Mariam found solace in small acts of reflection. A journal she kept, hidden under her pillow, became a space where she poured out her fears, triumphs, and prayers. It was here she wrote about a particularly haunting night when a young mother succumbed to the virus, leaving behind a crying infant. Fatimah a nurse on the ward took turns cradling the child, their tears mingling with whispered reassurances that seemed more for themselves than the baby. In Kota Kinabalu, on a Health Clinic care Johana's perspective on the pandemic began to shift dramatically. The collapse of the patient outside her clinic became a catalyst, forcing her to confront the stark reality of the virus's reach. As she adjusted to the new normal, Johana struggled to balance her professional responsibilities with her personal fears. Each day began with donning her protective gear and saying a silent prayer for strength. The clinic transformed into a frontline battleground as anxious patients sought answers and reassurance. Johana calmly accepted the facts Johana found unexpected strength in the small victories—a recovered patient, a successful referral to the hospital, or even a heartfelt thank-you from a stranger. These moments became her motivation, though they could not entirely erase the gnawing guilt of being apart from her family. Her evenings were spent on video calls, her children's laughter providing a fleeting respite from the weight of her isolation. The image of her elderly parents remained etched in her mind, a constant reminder of why she had chosen to protect them from her presence. As she neared retirement, Johana made the decision to return to her village permanently. She joined the rural health clinic as a consultant and spent her days teaching, treating, and inspiring the next generation. Her story came full circle when the baby she had delivered during her earlier stint at the clinic— now a young woman—approached her with aspirations of becoming a nurse. "You were the reason I wanted to do this," the young woman said, her eyes glistening with admiration. Johana felt her heart swell with pride, knowing her legacy would live on. Johana's journey is a testament to the power of resilience and the impact of unwavering dedication. From the bustling city hospitals to the quiet rural clinics, her story underscores the essence of healthcare: to heal, to connect, and to inspire. In the lush, diverse land of Sabah,. Another nurse beside the two by the name of Stella's resilience was a quiet, steadfast force that inspired those around her. The relentless demands of the hospital left no room for hesitation, yet within her, an unyielding determination burned. She began to see herself not just as a caregiver but as a guardian of hope—a beacon for those who were too weary to fight. Over time, her approach to each patient became more intuitive, her hands moving with precision, her voice steady and soothing.

Datuk Wilfred Lingham In stark contrast with the front runners, approached the pandemic from a position of relative stability and privilege. As the president of PPKS, his responsibilities were significant, but the lockdown merely altered the rhythm of his well-structured life. With access to resources and the foresight to prepare, he settled into a life of cautious adaptability. His spacious home became his sanctuary, a place where he could reflect on the events unfolding around lured viewed the pandemic through the lens of historical endurance. He had lived through turbulent times and learned the value of resilience. To him, this was yet another storm to weather. However, his perspective began to shift when he received news of old acquaintances succumbing to the virus. These losses brought a sobering realization—this crisis was not confined to statistics or distant news reports; it was deeply personal. Moved by the plight of healthcare workers, Wilfred initiated a plan to get all the twenty two district coordinating committe in the whole of Sabah to advise all members through PPKS, on the importance of keeping safe by adhering to the health ministry advice and to keep themselves safe by using mask at public places. He became a voice of support, often speaking out to encourage the community to adhere to safety measures. His actions, though removed from the direct frontline, offered a glimpse of solidarity, reminding healthcare workers that their efforts were not unnoticed. For Maimuna, Johana, and Wilfred, the pandemic was a shared yet uniquely personal journey. The frontliners bore the weight of direct confrontation with the virus, while Johana wrestled with the demands of care within a community setting. Wilfred's contribution lay in advocacy and support, a reminder that resilience took many forms. Their collective experiences painted a tapestry of Sabah's response to an unprecedented crisis—a story of courage, compassion, and unwavering hope. As the pandemic continued to unfold, each of them found ways to adapt, to contribute, and to persevere.

Datuk Wilfred Lingham

Maimona Johana and the rest of the gang often wondered what life would look like once the storm passed. They dreamed of reunions with family, of returning to a semblance of normalcy. For Wilfred, the pandemic served as a call to action, reinforcing the need for community and shared responsibility. Though their paths were different, their goals were the same: to ensure that Sabah emerged stronger, its spirit unbroken. And in the end, it was this shared determination that became the true hallmark of their stories.

As a pensioner Datuk Wilfred Lingham knew the community had changed in an instant. A leader who had seen his fair share of adversity, Wilfred, President of PPKS, approached life's challenges with calm precision. The COVID-19 pandemic, for him, seemed like a fleeting inconvenience—a brief disturbance in his well-ordered routine. Armed with his faith, a well-stocked pantry, and the protection of his vaccination, he believed he was ready for anything the virus could throw at him. But nothing could prepare him for what came next. A routine test, a simple precaution, delivered the shock of a lifetime: Wilfred was positive. The ground beneath him felt as if it had shifted. His unshakable confidence in his preparedness now seemed hollow in the face of the invisible threat of the virus. The sirens of the ambulance screamed in his ears as he was rushed to Queen Elizabeth Hospital, every second filled with rising panic. The sterile smell of the hospital was overpowering. The isolation room was cold, clinical, and, worse, it was a place where lives were lost. He entered the ward only to see a wrapped body being wheeled out on a gurney—death so close, so palpable that it left him breathless. As the door closed behind him, Wilfred was consumed with the terrifying thought: Was this how it was going to end for me? Days dragged on in a feverish haze. The symptoms, the isolation, the uncertainty— everything felt like an out-of-body experience. Every cough, every laboured breath felt like a reminder of his fragility. And yet, amid the fear, something remarkable began to happen. His X-rays showed progress, a hopeful sign. The shield of the vaccine, which had once seemed like just another part of routine, became his beacon of hope. The relief was slow, but it was there. After what felt like an eternity, the doctors finally discharged him, sending him home to quarantine.

Wilfred stepped outside, squinting against the harsh sunlight. He was alive—but what did that mean now? Months later, the impact of the pandemic still hung heavy over him. Finally, after his quarantine was over, he took leave and attended a short meeting at PPKS office.

Discussion at PPKS office

At a PPKS meeting, the weight of his experience bore down on him, showing on his weary face. He had always been a leader others looked to for guidance, but this time, the weariness wasn't just physical. He seemed different—a man whose heart had been changed by the brutal lessons of mortality.

In the PPKS office the room grew silent as Datuk Wilfred began came to chair a discussion to speak. His voice was steady but carried the weight of something deeper, something that had been haunting him since that fateful night. "It was a night like any other under the MCO," he began, his words measured but his gaze distant. "The weather was grim, the wind howling outside, battering the trees. I could hear them breaking, branches snapping under the pressure. It was almost as if nature itself was protesting. After dinner, I poured myself a glass of whisky, a habit from the past, and tried to unwind.

But I couldn't sleep. Around one in the morning, I woke to the sound of my neighbor's dog barking frantically. Something was wrong. "Wilfred paused, his hands shaking as he continued. "I moved toward the window, peering out into the darkness. What I saw made my heart stop. Two men—shadowy figures, desperate and quick—were trying to break into my cooler, stealing the fish I had spent weeks preparing for my wife's birthday. I was furious. with the thieves Those fish were a gift, an offering of love, a celebration of family. But then, something inside me snapped. "He stopped for a moment, his eyes clouded with the memory. "I went for my gun. It was a reflex. In that moment, it felt like the only way to protect what was mine. But as I took aim, my hand trembled. These weren't strangers; they were my neighbors— men driven by hunger, by the crushing weight of poverty. Men like so many others in this land, struggling to survive in a system that had left them behind. "Wilfred's voice faltered. "I had the power to pull the trigger, to end it all right then and there. But I couldn't. I realized that taking a life over a few fish was not the answer. These were men who were probably living in fear themselves, just trying to get by. Some of them were PTIs, people with no rights, no future. I couldn't be the one to make their suffering worse. "The room was still. The words hung in the air, and we all understood. Wilfred's story was not just about a man facing a moral dilemma—it was a window Into the struggles of the most vulnerable in society. The pandemic had not only ravaged the body but also deepened the divide between the haves and the have-nots. For many, survival meant choosing between desperation and moral compromise. Wilfred lowered his head, his fingers running through his greying hair. "I returned to my bed that night, my mind spinning. I didn't sleep. I couldn't. I was caught between anger and relief. I felt a sense of guilt for not protecting my family, but I also felt relieved that I hadn't taken a life in the heat of the moment. But most of all, I felt… I don't know… empty. "The room was quiet for a long time. We all knew what he was saying. The pandemic had exposed a deeper truth about the world we lived in. It wasn't just about the virus. It was about empathy, about survival, about the harsh realities people faced every day. "As we move toward recovery," Wilfred finally said, his voice strong but calm, "let us remember the lessons of this time. Compassion, not anger, must guide us. We are not just recovering from a virus—we are recovering from a broken system that has left too many behind. Let us rebuild, not just our economy, but our humanity. "In the months and years to come, Wilfred's story would echo across Sabah. It would serve as a reminder that leadership isn't just about making decisions—it's about the choices we make in the face of moral crossroads. It was a moment that defined him, and in that moment, he chose empathy. He chose to see beyond the anger, beyond the traction, and into the humanity of those who were suffering alongside him. Sabah emerged from the pandemic's shadow, it would be the stories of compassion, of people like Datuk Wilfred Lingham, that would help heal the wounds and guide the way forward. His leadership, shaped by vulnerability and compassion, would show the people of Sabah the true meaning of resilience.

Despite COVID-19, the 100th anniversary celebration of Holy Trinity School Tawau was celebrated with former Director of Education, Dr. Datuk Sri Hasbullah, gracing the occasion, in Kota Kinabalu

The 100 years Holy Trinity anniversary celebration was accompanied by a well know band called Midnight flyers led by the late Mahmood Kalong and evergreen unlimited Country Band lead by Datuk Ladislaus Maluda

In a nut shell how Covid 19 disrupted society, isolating senior citizen, burdening housewife's, devasting farmers, hawkers and fisherman. Self-employed professionals face income loss, while small business struggled to adapt. Supply chains collapsed, labour shortages arose, and financial insecurity spread leaving all sectors -from families to the working class-grappling with uncertainty and unprecedented challenges. Here are some of the untold stories:

As Johan, an active lad found out one morning. He woke up late and jumped out of bed as fast as he could. His alarm clock had failed him, mother stood beside the bed, armed with a glass of cool water for a morning call. Just as she was about to administer her wake-up method, Johan woke up in the nick of time to avoid her deed. In a jiffy, with no time to spare, he rushed through his morning ritual before beginning his journey to school. Off he went down the unpaved track that led to the hanging bridge.

Hanging bridge Johan needs to pass daily even after 61 years after Malaysia

With his heavy school bag on his back, he cautiously jumped over the ridge onto the bridge proper, a feat he had performed many times before. He was mindful of the risks and dangers, walking watchfully as he maneuverer across the flimsy bridge. He carefully avoided the several rotten, retired wooden planks that clung precariously to the cable railing attached at both ends of the river bank.

Below the bridge, the rushing sound of the swollen river was audible, amplified by the heavy rain the night before. A fall would mean a sad ending, as the river teemed with fish and harboured several reptiles. Years ago, several deaths had occurred when the fell admits the swollen river during rainy days. due to the unforgiving sweep of the stream. Once across the bridge, Johan felt at ease. He took a piece of bread and ate his breakfast. Barely had he finished eating when the rickety old bus arrived. Along the way, he caught a glimpse of his parents toiling in the field, working from dawn to dusk. "I need to study hard," he lamented. "I need to break free from the backbreaking farming work of my ancestors. "The other kids on the bus chattered and laughed joyfully as the driver struggled to avoid the potholes along the road. The weather was accommodating, with birds flying among the trees. As they reached the school, the bell was ringing loudly. They arrived just in time before the school gate closed.

Back home at 7:00 PM, Johan did his homework before finishing off for the day. Math was his most challenging subject. Both of his parents were illiterate, and no one at home could help him. Three of his siblings had left the comfort of the village seeking greener pastures. Two had gone overseas to work, and one was in Kota Kinabalu. Kota Kinabalu was once a utopia town, but since our neighbouring country was involved in insurrection many escaped to our little town. Since then, development in the town was hampered by various reasons under the sun. Our young men and women had to travel elsewhere to fine opportunities to secure their futures. For the last five years, Johan had struggled with his schoolwork, but it did not deter him from trying hard. He longed for term breaks, a chance to have fun with his friends.

In February 2020, Johan's wishful thinking was unexpectedly answered. The bell rang, and the children were asked to assemble immediately. At the assembly, they were told to return home; school would be closed until further notice. Johan was filled with joy but also perplexed—their school break was still far off. As they passed through town on their way home, they noticed many shops were closed, and few people were loitering around. Police officers and others wore masks everywhere. Reaching his home in Tongod village, Johan was surprised to see no one in sight. The door to his house was closed. The moment he reached home, his mother was waiting at the door with her mask on. She ushered him inside and told him to take a shower. Johan's mind was in confusion, trying to make sense of the situation.

A month passed, and there was still no word from the school.Johan was thrilled and happy, anticipating the extra time he would have with his friends. However, his parents did not share his enthusiasm. They were concerned that his education might be in jeopardy. Additionally, they needed to tend to their stalls to sell produce from their garden.Several months passed, and children were asked to learn online. Unfortunately, most of the kampong houses lacked internet connections or computers.The only available online learning resources were quite a distance away.Poor Johan had no choice but to refer to his textbooks and study by himself. Those with the right tools still had opportunities, but online learning was a new phenomenon and very challenging for students in Sabah. This system was exacerbated by unreliable WIFI connections and power disruptions. For students to fully understand and utilize these new methods was a daunting task. Furthermore, remote villages in Sabah lacked most modern facilities, including proper internet connections A recent story in the local news highlighted a girl who had to endanger herself by climbing to the top of a tree just to get proper WIFI reception. This highlighted the severe limitations faced by students in these areas. ver since we joined Malaysia, our communication infrastructure has not been fully realized. It will probably take years before our dream can come true. While the rest of the world has made profound advancements, we are still lagging behind in many ways due to lack of conscientious and honesty from the past leadership

School-going students found their routines disrupted and restlessness grew with each passing day of absence. Initially a novelty, extended time at home soon left them yearning for the structure and camaraderie of school. Amidst escalating challenges, the Ministry of Education ventured into uncharted territory with online learning, a glimpse into the future of education.

Online learning by students

Technology emerged as the cornerstone of future learning processes, shaping a new era for students. "In towns, where exposure came earlier, individuals had a better chance to succeed in adapting to new circumstances. However, for those living in remote kampongs, the task was daunting. Poor WIFI connections and signal interruptions plagued their efforts, making mastery of online learning a significant challenge for any. Only time will reveal the true measure of success for this project." This version emphasizes the contrast between urban and rural challenges in adapting to online learning during the pandemic, highlighting the specific difficulties faced by those in remote areas due to connectivity issues.

Meanwhile in the agriculture sector, several farmers were caught in a web of the COVID-19 scenario, as Joseph and Andrew's lives were turned upside down. Once thriving in their small rural community, the two farmers found themselves grappling with challenges they had never anticipated. The pandemic not only disrupted their daily routines but also cast uncertainty over their livelihood and future.

Joseph, a seasoned vegetable farmer, relied heavily on local markets to sell his produce. However, with movement restrictions and lockdowns in place, these markets were shut down or operating at minimal capacity. Tons of fresh vegetables went unsold, leaving Joseph staring at piles of rotting produce. The sight of his hard work wasted was heartbreaking. He had invested everything—time, labor, and resources—but the pandemic left him with mounting debts and dwindling hope.

Andrew, on the other hand, was a livestock farmer who supplied poultry to nearby towns. His challenges were no less severe. The closure of restaurants, hotels, and school cafeterias caused a sharp decline in demand for his chickens. Feed costs, however, continued to rise, as supply chain disruptions made it difficult to import essential agricultural goods. With every passing day, Andrew struggled to keep his farm running. His barns, once bustling with activity, now felt eerily quiet.

For Joseph and Andrew, the pandemic was more than a health crisis; it was a test of resilience and survival. Support from government initiatives or local cooperatives became their only lifeline. They began exploring alternative ways to sustain themselves—Joseph tried delivering vegetables directly to customers, while Andrew turned to online platforms to market his poultry.

Their story echoes the plight of countless farmers during the pandemic. The struggle to adapt to a rapidly changing world reshaped not just their business practices, but also their outlook on life and community. In the face of adversity, Joseph and Andrew learned to embrace innovation and solidarity, proving that even the harshest challenges could inspire new beginnings.

In the agricultural and plantation sectors of large plantati9on, many lost their incomes due to the scarcity of workers, a situation exacerbated by COVID-19. Small farmers like Joseph in Kundasang, who worked alone with his family on their modest plot, managed to sustain their daily needs. Joseph's farm was a small, family-run operation that didn't require additional Labor; his wife and children helped him with the chores. He was so engrossed in his work that he rarely kept up with the news affecting the world. One sunny morning, Joseph happily loaded his fresh produce onto his old basket and headed to the rows of stall to sell it. The heavy basket bounced on his shoulders along the dusty road, the sky clear above, promising a good day of sales. However, his journey was abruptly halted by a group of stern-faced policemen. They informed him that he had broken the Movement Control Order (MCO). Perplexed and uneducated about the new regulations, Joseph was bewildered by the commotion. He was not alone; several other farmers found themselves in the same predicament. After recording his identification, the police instructed him to report to the station and pay a fine of one thousand ringgits. Joseph was at a loss. His savings, a modest sum kept in a bamboo jar by his wife and children, were nowhere near enough to cover the fine. Desperate, Joseph went to see his village chief and explained his situation. The village chief, moved by Joseph's plight, decided to gather the villagers to explain the current situation. The community, bound by solidarity, collected money to help Joseph pay his fine. The next day, Joseph, with trembling hands, counted out the coins and crumpled notes in front of a police officer. The officer, witnessing the farmer's struggle, felt a pang of guilt. Here was a poor man, compounded just for trying to sell his goods in town. The officer told Joseph to give eight hundred ringgits, assuring him that he would cover the rest. Overwhelmed with relief, Joseph thanked the policeman for his kindness. It was a small gesture that revealed the soft hearts that still existed in times of trouble. Meanwhile, the Ministry of Health recorded more infections across several clusters, and the number of deaths increased dramatically. It was a calamity that struck at the very core of society, taking away ordinary people who had once been vibrant and alive. The stark reality of lives suddenly extinguished was hard to fathom. Could we protect ourselves from the unseen enemies lurking in every corner of our living spaces? Daily, the media bombarded us with advice on how to shield ourselves from the hidden virus. The guidance was sound, but ultimately, adherence lay in the hands of each individual. Joseph's story, like many others during this crisis, became a testament to the human spirit's resilience and compassion. The lockdown had brought communities closer, revealing the strength found in unity and the kindness that emerged in the face of adversity. As the days turned into months, the world grappled with the pandemic's relentless grip, each person navigating their own path through the uncertainty, hoping for a return to a semblance of normalcy. Andrew meanwhile has transformed his poultry farming to vegetable farming and was preparing to sell his product in the tamu ground. The enterprising farmer, had meticulously arranged his bountiful produce in the wicker basket, a culmination of six months of hard work and anticipation. Each fruit and vegetable were placed with care, a testament to his dedication and hope for a profitable day ahead. With a satisfied smile, he set off down the familiar path, whistling a tune that echoed his contentment. Yet, as he approached his usual spot in the bustling marketplace, he noticed something amiss. Instead of the usual throngs of eager customers, there were rows of police and security personnel, bustling about with purposeful urgency, carrying out government directives. Perplexed but undeterred, Andrew pressed forward, eager to set up his stall and begin selling his prized produce. However, his path was abruptly blocked by a stern-faced police officer who signalled for him to halt and turn back. Politely, yet firmly, the officer gestured towards the directive, urging Andrew to comply and not set up his stall today. Irritation flickered across Andrew's face as he tried to reason with the officer, pleading for just a moment to sell his goods nearby. His voice was adamant, fuelled by a mix of frustration and determination to make the best of the day. The scene unfolded against the backdrop of Andrew's vivid hopes and the stark reality of unexpected circumstances, creating a tension between his aspirations and the enforced regulations. Andrew, the determined farmer, stood his ground despite the polite but firm refusals from the police officer. Each request to turn back was met with stubborn resistance as Andrew argued vehemently, his frustration palpable in the crisp morning air. Tempers flared in the heated exchange; the officer increasingly annoyed by Andrew's persistent appeals. Finally, exasperated by the farmer's defiance, the officer reached for his pen, swiftly jotting down a summons. With a terse motion, he handed the slip of paper to Andrew, who snatched it rudely and shoved it into his pocket, his face contorted with anger. Turning away from the marketplace, Andrew trudged back home with his basket still brimming with unsold produce. The weight of disappointment hung heavy on his shoulders, exacerbated by his ignorance of the unfolding crisis due to COVID-19 in Sabah. His arguments earlier stemmed from a primal need—the right to earn a livelihood by selling his hard-earned harvest. Back home, his wife, expecting good news, was bewildered by the sight of him returning empty-handed. Andrew collapsed onto a stool, his demeanour pathetic and defeated. With a trembling voice, he recounted the morning's events, struggling to explain the abrupt turn of events and the crushing blow to their hopes. The vivid scene painted a poignant picture of resilience and shattered expectations, capturing the clash between personal ambition and unforeseen circumstances in the throes of a larger societal crisis. Andrew, still reeling from the events of the morning, retrieved the crumpled summons from his worn pants pocket and cautiously unfolded it. His eyes widened in disbelief as he scanned the neatly printed charge— a hefty thousand ringgit fine. The weight of the amount hit him like a physical blow, leaving him stunned and speechless. Fury surged within Andrew as he crudely cursed the officer in his mind, blaming him for the unexpected financial burden. Regret washed over him as he realized his own heated argument had precipitated this costly consequence. His earlier defiance now seemed reckless and ill-advised. Sitting in the dim light of his home, Andrew grappled with the daunting reality. How could he possibly raise such a significant sum? The inability to sell his produce in the market compounded his worries, threatening his daily income and livelihood. Facing two existential crises—the looming fine and the stall closure— Andrew found himself on the brink of despair. Sleep evaded him that night, his mind churning with anxiety and uncertainty. By morning, he resolved to seek help from the native chief, hoping against hope for a solution to his dire predicament. The weight of responsibility and the consequences of his actions bore heavily on him, painting a vivid picture of a man at the mercy of circumstance, grappling with the repercussions of a single, fateful decision Andrew, still reeling from the morning's turmoil, retrieved the crumpled summons from his worn pants pocket. With trembling hands, he unfolded the paper under the dim glow of a kerosene lamp, revealing the stark reality of a thousand-ringgit fine. The figure loomed large in the small, modest room, casting a shadow over his already troubled thoughts. Bitterness welled up inside Andrew as he silently cursed the officer who had issued the summons. His mind raced with crude epithets aimed at the uniformed figure whose stern demeanour had now translated into a severe financial penalty. Yet, amidst the anger, a pang of remorse gnawed at him as he acknowledged that his own obstinate argument had brought about this harsh consequence. In the quiet of his home, with only the faint sounds of crickets outside, Andrew sat with his back against the wall. The weight of the fine pressed upon him, magnified by the realization that his poultry farm and vegetable stall, his source of income, was now under threat. Unable to sell his chicken and meticulously grown produce at the market, he faced not only the loss of earnings but also the uncertainty of how to pay such a sum. As the night stretched on, sleep eluded him, replaced instead by anxious thoughts and restless pacing. With each passing hour, his resolve hardened—he would seek counsel from the village chief, the native leader respected for his wisdom and guidance in times of crisis. Andrew's hope flickered faintly against the backdrop of impending hardship, painting a vivid portrait of resilience amidst adversity in the heart of the rural community. Meanwhile in another tamu ground, as dusk settled, the women bustling at the tamu ground in a small village we're getting ready to depart. Among them were spirited housewives and enterprising traders, their stalls brimming with fresh produce. The tamu was their cherished rendezvous—a vibrant hub where they shared tales, caught up with old acquaintances, and indulged in the day's juiciest gossip. Oblivious to the distant havoc wrought by the Covid-19 pandemic, they revelled in the warmth of community and camaraderie.""Amidst the bustling routines of village life, Mariam and her husband prepared to wind down after a gruelling twelve-hour day at the market. The following morning, they eagerly set off on their usual route, only to notice an unsettling tranquillity—a stark contrast to the usual lively crowds. Few souls hurried about their morning chores, and an unusual presence of security officer forces added to their unease. Approaching a junction, they were flagged down by police officers, prompting a cautious U-turn. Jagan, troubled but keeping his thoughts to himself, felt a sense of foreboding throughout the journey. The evening brought an eerie calm to their dinner table, shattered by the sudden ring of the phone—an update from their daughter on the pandemic's devastating global impact. As they dined, Mariam noticed her husband's anxiety dissipate with the news, though he remained quiet. Later, just before bed, he savoured his Favorite local brew, finding solace in its familiar taste amidst the uncertainty. "He slept soundly until the early hours of the morning, cocooned in a deep slumber undisturbed by the world outside. Days turned into weeks, then months, and still, there was no sign of the Movement Control Order (MCO) being lifted. They were confined to their small house, marooned amidst the unfolding pandemic. Jagan spent his days toiling in his plot of land until the sun dipped below the horizon. With a small poultry and vegetable garden, they managed to eke out a living, sustaining themselves amidst the global pandemic that continued its relentless sweep. The prolonged extension of the COVID-19 restrictions weighed heavily on the people of Sabah, especially those relying on daily wages. Their savings dwindled day by day, casting a shadow of uncertainty over their future. Yet, amidst the apprehension, resilience prevailed among the natives. They were determined to survive against all odds, drawing lessons from past hardships like the Second World War. Nearby jungles and river offered additional resources to sustain them through these challenging times. Fortunately, NGOs joined hands with the government to distribute essential supplies, providing a lifeline to the community. Beside the farmers a young, enterprising entrepreneur brimmed with optimism, his heart alight with the promise of a bright future. He had recently embarked on the ambitious journey of starting his own studio, driven by a fervent desire for independence and self-reliance after years of toiling for a company in the same industry. His new office was a sanctuary of creativity and innovation, adorned with sleek furniture, the latest technology, and walls plastered with motivational quotes. Each morning, he entered this space with a sense of purpose, imagining the flourishing enterprise that lay ahead. However, his aspirations were brutally shattered when COVID-19 swept across the nation like an unrelenting storm, leaving him saddled with debt and uncertainty. This is his story. The young man, fuelled by boundless passion and hope, had invested every ounce of his resources and energy into his nascent venture. He envisioned a future where his hard work and creativity would culminate in success and recognition. But now, his future hung precariously in the balance. The once bustling streets outside his studio were now eerily silent, the vibrant cityscape reduced to a ghost town. It could take months, or even years, for life to return to normalcy. Alongside him, several of his friends found themselves grappling with the same dire scenario. Among them was a young executive by the name of Alfred, a visionary with grand ambitions of becoming a successful advertising mogul. With a wealth of experience under his belt, he had boldly left his former company and launched a parallel business, envisioning a venture that would reflect his innovative spirit. His office, a hub of creativity and dynamic energy, thrummed with the excitement and dedication of his newly assembled team. To kickstart his enterprise, he had taken out a substantial loan, employing a cadre of talented individuals to help realize his vision. For several months, everything seemed to be progressing splendidly. The business thrived, attracting a steady stream of clients and garnering enthusiastic praise. The young executive was filled with pride and optimism, confident that his company was on an unstoppable trajectory towards a bright future. Each day, he revelled in the challenges and opportunities that came his way, certain that success was within reach. One evening, as the last door of his vibrant office closed and the city skyline transitioned into a serene twilight, he returned home to his family, seeking solace and rest. After a warm, hearty dinner, he settled into his favorite armchair to watch the national news, a daily ritual that provided a semblance of routine and stability. He had heard murmurs of the mysterious disease originating in Wuhan China but had dismissed it, convinced that it would soon be contained and forgotten.

Little did he know, his optimism would soon be met with a harsh and unyielding reality. The pandemic was not just a distant threat but an imminent catastrophe that would upend his life and shatter his dreams. As the news reports grew increasingly dire, the impact on his business was immediate and devastating. Projects were abruptly cancelled, clients vanished, and the once bustling office fell into an eerie silence.

The city, which once pulsed with endless opportunities, now seemed to close in on him, a stark reminder of dreams deferred and futures uncertain. The young executive, like many others, found himself navigating an uncharted landscape of adversity, where the path to recovery seemed fraught with challenges and uncertainties. As he gazed out of his window, the city lights flickering in the distance, he couldn't help but reflect on the fragility of dreams and the unpredictable nature of life. The pandemic had not only disrupted his professional aspirations but had also underscored the resilience and adaptability required to weather such unprecedented times. His story, like that of many others, became a testament to the indomitable human spirit and the relentless pursuit of hope, even in the face of overwhelming odds.Out of the blue came the shattering, breaking news directly from the Prime Minister of Malaysia that caught Alex by surprise. A piece of news that sent shudders down his spine, a blow from which he feared he might never recover: A NATIONAL LOCKDOWN FOR TWO WEEKS. The lockdown threatened to disrupt his meticulously laid plans, a bitter pill that sent his mind into disarray. Alex tried to remain calm and assess the situation, his mind racing as he pondered how to navigate this unforeseen crisis. That night turned into the worst nightmare Alex had ever encountered. The loan he had taken from the bank loomed large in his thoughts, with its monthly payments hanging over him like a guillotine. Without his daily income, he was staring down a financial abyss. The next morning, Alex went to the office with a heavy heart to inform his staff of the devastating news: the company would need to wind down. As he delivered the grim announcement, he saw the shock and despair in their eyes, mirroring his own fears. Then, in the afternoon, another bombshell dropped. The foreign company he had heavily relied upon had also shut down due to the coronavirus. With no lifeline to cling to, Alex had no choice but to suspend his staff until further notice and sell all the furniture and equipment for a fraction of their value to recoup some reserves. With limited options, Alex could only hope for the best and pray for a return to normalcy.

The COVID-19 situation in Malaysia worsened, with the lockdown creating a massive impact across every front of society. The tourism industry, once a vibrant cornerstone of the economy, crumbled as flights were grounded and borders closed. The airline industry, employing thousands, was hit hard, leading to widespread job losses. The ripple effect of COVID-19 put millions out of work across every sector. A silent cry of despair echoed from the local population, who found themselves without means to sustain their livelihoods. The newly formed government swiftly announced a RM 250 billion stimulus package, but for many, the uncertainty remained overwhelming.

Alex gazed out of his apartment window, the cityscape bathed in an eerie quiet. The bustling streets he once knew were empty, the vibrancy of life replaced by a stillness that felt almost surreal. He reflected on the fragility of his dreams and the precarious nature of life itself. Each day brought new challenges, and the weight of responsibility pressed heavily on his shoulders. He longed for a return to the days when his biggest concern was meeting client deadlines, not the survival of his business and the welfare of his employees.As weeks turned into months, Alex adapted to the new normal, finding small ways to keep his spirit and his dreams alive. He reached out to clients, explored new business models, and leaned on the support of friends and family. The journey was arduous, filled with setbacks and moments of doubt, but Alex's resilience and determination never wavered. The pandemic had taught him harsh lessons about vulnerability and strength, about the unpredictability of life and the power of hope. His story, like that of so many others, became a testament to the enduring human spirit, to the courage and tenacity that shine brightest in the darkest times.

Despite the government's efforts, disgruntled voices echoed from every sector of society. Was this a day of reckoning, a wake-up call to rethink our unsustainable lifestyle and our daily consumption of the Earth's natural resources? Deep soul-searching and repentance seemed necessary to save our only home. Next to his building stood a small shop mained by a veteran shopkeeper For Ah Seng, an elderly shopkeeper in Kampong Air, life took a cruel turn as the pandemic shuttered his once-thriving shop. Dependent on tourism, particularly visitors from China, his income dried up overnight. The bustling crowds that once filled his shop with chatter and commerce were replaced by an eerie silence. With bills to pay and family to support, he faced the agonizing reality of dwindling resources and uncertain prospects. Each of these individuals navigated the pandemic's upheaval with resilience and determination, their lives forever altered by circumstances beyond their control. Their stories reflect the stark realities faced by many in Sabah, where livelihoods hang in the balance and hopes hinge on the promise of a return to normalcy that remains elusive. At the onset of the outbreak, Ah Seng's shop in Kampong Air bustled with life as tourists from China frequented his establishment, exchanging stories and laughter. Unaware of the looming danger, he relished these interactions, blissfully oblivious to the invisible threat that lurked among his clientele. Then, like a sudden storm on a tranquil day, symptoms struck. Coughs wracked Ah Seng's frail body, stealing his breath in suffocating gasps. Panic gripped him and his wife as they realized the gravity of their situation. Days blurred into a haze of uncertainty as they fought against the relentless assault of the virus, their fate hanging precariously in the balance. Around the globe, the pandemic's grip tightened, leaving millions feeling powerless in its wake. Ah Seng's plight mirrored that of countless others, a stark reminder of the indiscriminate havoc wreaked by the virus. In this tumultuous time, hope flickered dimly on the horizon, a fragile beacon amidst the chaos. Now, as the world collectively strives to contain and conquer the pandemic, each day becomes a battle for survival. Ah Seng's story serves as a poignant reminder of our shared vulnerability and the urgent need for unity and resolve in the face of an unprecedented crisis.

As the pandemic continued unabated, many blue and daily workers were greatly affected in their daily lives Encik Paulus and his colleagues, the abrupt halt of their daily routine was equally bewildering. With no clear explanation from their employer, they found themselves abruptly sent home, isolated from their livelihoods and left to fend for themselves. Stranded in a small jungle village, Paulus sought solace in reconnecting with friends, navigating blocked roads and sparse supplies to find moments of normalcy amidst the chaos. Gathered in a makeshift kongsi, they shared stories over coffee, piecing together the fragments of information about the pandemic that had upended their lives. Paulus, like many, struggled to comprehend the gravity of the situation, but in the company of friends, found fleeting respite from the isolation and uncertainty that gripped the world outside. a migrant worker from Indonesia, found himself stranded and deeply worried about his family back home. Cut off from his regular income and with rations dwindling, he faced mounting uncertainty. The abrupt halt in his employer's support compounded his anxiety, leaving him with little choice but to rely on sporadic food drives that offered temporary relief. Despite this, his thoughts never strayed far from his loved ones, yearning for the day he could reunite with them, contingent upon the uncertain course of the pandemic Amidst the country's battle against COVID-19, in Penampang nature, oblivious to human strife, unleashed its wrath. Sheets of rain poured relentlessly for days, quenching the earth's thirst but unwittingly plunging low-lying areas into chaos. The deluge transformed streets into turbulent rivers, submerging homes and villages under murky waters. Families scrambled to evacuate to makeshift shelters in community centres or any dry refuge they could find. Emergency services strained under the dual burden of pandemic and flood, racing to aid the displaced populace. In the midst of this watery onslaught, a two-story house stood defiantly against the floodwaters, spared but not untouched. Inside, the inundation wreaked havoc, rendering appliances useless and prized possessions ruined. As night fell, darkness enveloped the landscape. Power outage plunged affected areas into obscurity, leaving only those with solar lights to navigate cautiously through the gloom. Others resorted to flickering torches and the warm glow of candles, their flickering light casting eerie shadows amidst the rising waters. Amidst this chaos, fears of lurking dangers intensified. The threat of snakes and other hazards lurked in the shadows, forcing families to remain vigilant even as they sought safety from the floodwaters. Amidst the aftermath, the Chief Minister voiced frustrations over funds allocated years ago to prevent such calamities, now seemingly vanished without a trace. The proposed monsoon drainage system, conceived years ago, lay dormant through seasons, leaving the community vulnerable. The inadequate infrastructure struggled to cope with the deluge, exacerbated by blocked drains hindering smooth water flow submerging everything on its path. Mary a housewife, found herself stranded atop her dining table, seeking refuge from the relentless onslaught of debris-laden mud water that breached her home through the open door. The sudden flash flood wreaked havoc across the small community. Mary's neighbour, just a stone's throw away, faced a similar plight. Alone in her husband's absence, she struggled to salvage household items amidst rising waters, finally seeking safety by leaping onto her elevated bed, watching helplessly as her living room flooded. The adversity was widespread. Many homes in their vicinity bore the brunt of the calamity, their interiors submerged in murky floodwaters. Further down in Donggonon hamlet, chaos reigned as the flash flood turned streets into temporary lakes. Heavy vehicles ploughed through the waterlogged roads while lighter vehicles remained stranded, their drivers bravely attempting to navigate unseen waterways. Tragically, amidst the chaos, lives were lost. Drivers, miscalculating the depth of the floodwaters, fell victim to the relentless river's currents. Oswald, another friend just looked on with his ukulele on his hand trampling any song he could find, witnessing the recurring flood. With every storm. His property in the flood-prone area resembled a sanctuary for crocodiles, submerged under water. Frustrated, he lashed out at his elected representative who had promised action during elections but conveniently forgot afterward, leaving promises unfulfilled and grievances ignored once the votes were cast. Politicians had been making promises for the past two decades to address the flooding issue, yet all that remained was an incomplete monsoon drain, a stark symbol of unfulfilled commitments. When questioned, politicians conjured up countless reasons and excuses, resulting in projects allocated with funds that languished for decades without completion. Amidst the backdrop of the ongoing COVID-19 pandemic, a political cataclysm unfolded, driven by human ambition. It began at the federal level, where several avaricious politicians from the ruling state government unexpectedly declared their support for the opposition. This seismic shift in allegiance created a volatile situation within the government. Swiftly, the state assembly was dissolved and elections were called, despite the country still grappling with the pandemic. After the general election for parliament completed, The turmoil at the federal level heated up. Finally, a resolution was found through the intervention of the King, after extensive consultations with all concerned parties.

The people of the sea

Meanwhile in Semporna prefecture the tribe of the sea were caught in a precarious position when they were stopped by the health ministry.

The People of the Sea, often referred to as the Pelahu or the lost tribe of Borneo, inhabit the coastlines of Southeast Asia. Once a thriving community, their population has significantly dwindled over the years due to the encroachment of modern society. A new generation has emerged, gradually abandoning their ancestral way of life. In their heyday, the Pelahu were celebrated for their adventurous spirit. They roamed the high seas, living on tiny boats called lipa lipa, each no larger than twenty-five square meters. For them, the sea was their world, and the sky their roof. Their lives were a continuous journey across the vast waters of Southeast Asia, hopping from island to island in search of fresh water or to bury their dead. Their existence was fraught with danger from treacherous weather and the ever-present threat of the sea. Armed with homemade spears, they dived deep into the ocean to hunt for food, spending several minutes underwater to secure meals that would last them for days.

Illiterate and unexposed to the modern world, they survived entirely on what nature provided. When the COVID-19 pandemic struck the world, the Pelahu remained untouched by the virus, their isolated way of life shielding them from the global chaos. They travelled in clusters of boats for safety, rarely venturing onto land unless absolutely necessary. Storms and the growl of the sea often forced them to seek refuge on nearby islands or in coastal villages. They knew their little vessels couldn't withstand brewing storms, so they would quickly sail to safer havens to protect their families. In 2021, the tribe faced an unprecedented ordeal. Forced ashore, they were caught in the chaos of a pandemic screening program. The health department, on high alert due to the rampant spread of COVID-19, conducted rigorous tests on everyone. The Pelahu, bewildered and frightened, tried to evade the authorities but were swiftly detained and escorted to examination centres' these sea gypsies, the detention was a harrowing experience. Children cried, and women desperately tried to escape the clutches of the authorities. They were herded into a small, guarded hut for further health evaluations. After several days, they were released, some barely able to walk due to the confinement. As they made their way back to their boats, they witnessed several burials at cemeteries, a stark reminder of the pandemic's deadly toll. With heavy hearts and a sense of foreboding, they slipped away into the deep blue sea, vanishing from sight, never to be seen again. Their departure was a silent protest against a world that had grown too intrusive, too dangerous. The Pelahu returned to the vast, indifferent ocean, seeking solace in the sea sanctuary.

Unity and Hope Define Sabah's Post-Pandemic Spirit.

The final days of COVID-19 in Sabah marked a transition from crisis to cautious normalcy. Restrictions eased, and life resumed as businesses reopened, schools returned to face-to-face learning, and tourism rebounded in iconic destinations like Mount Kinabalu and Sipadan Island. Accelerated vaccination campaigns, even in remote areas, reduced severe cases, helping the state move toward endemicity. Community resilience shone brightly as locals supported each other, strengthened bonds, and learned vital lessons about healthcare, digital education, and food security. Memorials honoured those lost to the virus, while Sabahans celebrated their regained freedoms with a renewed sense of responsibility. Emerging from the pandemic, Sabah stood as a beacon of unity, adaptability, and hope, ready to rebuild and embrace a brighter future.

The Sabah State Government Pensioners Association has initiated a new committee to tackle challenges and improve programs for seniors.

The Genesis and Evolution of the Sabah Government Pensioners Association.

In 1998, over a casual coffee discussion, Mr. Terance Liau, Mr. Stephen Chin, Mr. Lee Ming Tet, and Mr. Ho Wing Yau mooted the idea of forming an association dedicated to Sabah government pensioners. Their vision became a reality on December 29, 1998, when they received official accreditation from the Registrar of Societies.

Sitting L-R: *Dennis Lim (Asst. Secretary), *Philip Liew (Vice President), Terence Liau (President), Stephen Chin (Secretary), Philip Ng (Treasurer)*

Standing: *Liew Kim Fatt (Asst. Treasurer), Alan Koh (Member), David Woo (Member), Peter Koh (Member), and Chin Kim Phin (Member)*

The journey, however, was not without challenges. In its early stages, the movement progressed slowly, struggling to entice pensioners to participate. Despite limited financial support from the government, the founders exhibited resilience and determination, sustaining the association through membership fees and personal contributions.

ting L-R: *Dennis Lim (Asst. Secretary), Chin Kim Phin (Member), Ho Wing Yau (Coordinator), Terence Liau (President), Doris Yeo Bee Lian (Coordinator), Mary Voo (Coordinator), Philip Liew (Vice President)*

anding *Philip Ng (Treasurer), Liew Kim Fatt (Asst. Treasurer), Alan Koh (Member), Stephen Chin (Secretary), Peter Thien Yin Ken (Coordinator), David Woo (Member), John Lai (Coordinator) and Peter Koh (Member)*

The formation of the proem committee marked a turning point, enabling the association to extend its reach to major towns such as Sandakan and Tawau. Although resources were scarce, the committee embarked on visits to these towns, explaining the benefits of joining the association. The government eventually allocated office space at Maksak, allowing the association to operate on a daily basis. As funds grew, a temporary clerk was employed to manage memberships and process applications from interested pensioners.

In the association's first general meeting, Mr. Terance Liau was confirmed as its inaugural president. However, in the following general meeting, Mr. Liau decided not to seek re-election. Two groups contested the leadership: one led by Dr. Epin and the other by Datuk Godfrey Lim. Ultimately, Dr. Epin was elected president, and under his leadership, the association continued its work, albeit with modest membership growth.

During Dr. Epin's tenure, the committee proposed joining the Perkhidmatan Majlis Masyarakat Sabah (MPMS). Their application was approved on December 20, 2009, granting the association limited financial assistance. Although this funding provided some relief, it was insufficient to expand activities significantly.

A transformative chapter began on December 24, 2019, when Datuk Wilfred Lingham assumed leadership. Consolidating his position, Datuk Wilfred introduced a new direction for the association.

the President had to reach out to pensioners in Labuan

He established the Administrative Finance Outreach (AFO) committee and nominated outstanding and experienced members to contribute fresh ideas to spur the activities of the association. One of his significant initiatives was the creation of District Coordinating Committees (DCCs) in every major town in Sabah. These DCCs aimed to engage pensioners at the grassroots level, increasing membership substantially.By 2024, the association had grown to over 5,000 members. With increased allocations from MPMS, the committee was able to visit DCCs regularly, promoting activities and addressing senior pensioners' health concerns.

An innovative idea to organize short seminars for soon-to-be retirees was also introduced, supported by funds raised through state government allocations.

The Sabah Government Pensioners Association continues to thrive, providing a platform for pensioners to engage, support one another, and advocate for their collective needs. Let us celebrate together 27 years of PPKS existence in 2025 The Sabah Pensioners Association (PPKS) proudly marks 27 years of service, championing the welfare and unity of pensioners across the state. From its modest beginnings, the association has faced significant challenges, including financial constraints and limited membership. However, through steadfast leadership and innovative strategies, PPKS has grown into a thriving organization that makes a real difference in the lives of its members.

A pivotal transformation occurred in 2019 under Datuk Wilfred Lingham's leadership, introducing a grassroots-driven approach with the formation of District Coordinating Committees (DCCs) across Sabah. This effort empowered local pensioners and created a sense of belonging, addressing issues more effectively at the community level. With the support of MPMS, the state government's welfare entity, PPKS further expanded its reach, organizing seminars, programs, and activities that directly benefit its members. Membership in PPKS is more than a formality—it's a commitment to collective strength and shared advocacy. Non-member pensioners are encouraged to join and take advantage of the many benefits the association offers PPKS serves as a united platform to amplify the voices of pensioners, ensuring their contributions to nation-building are recognized. By joining, members strengthen the association's ability to advocate for better policies, benefits, and programs that safeguard their dignity and welfare. Programs that support and tailored for pensioners through seminars, health programs, and community initiatives, PPKS ensures members stay active, informed, and well-supported. It also offers opportunities for members to share their experiences, knowledge, and camaraderie, building a stronger sense of community, Collaborating for Infrastructure and Care.

With a growing number of pensioners facing challenges in their golden years, PPKS actively engages with the government to address critical needs. Many pensioners, whose children are preoccupied with making their own living, often lack family support. By joining PPKS, members contribute to collective efforts aimed at urging the government to establish dedicated care centres and facilities for pensioners. Health and Well-Being as Priorities Pension funds allocated to retirees should be utilized not just for sustenance but also to ensure access to proper healthcare and medical facilities. PPKS advocates for policies that prioritize pensioners' health, enabling them to enjoy their retirement with dignity and security. PPKS believes that the government plays a crucial role in supporting pensioners during their golden years. Beyond financial aid, it is essential to develop infrastructure that caters to their unique needs. Dedicated care centres for pensioners can provide professional support, companionship, and medical attention, ensuring that retirees do not have to depend entirely on their children for welfare. These centres would offer pensioners a safe and nurturing environment, allowing their families to focus on their own livelihoods without guilt calls for more proactive measures, such as increasing healthcare subsidies, ensuring pensioners have access to affordable medication, and supporting wellness programs that promote a healthy lifestyle. A government-pensioner partnership can create a robust system where retirees are celebrated for their contributions and assured of a comfortable life after years of dedicated service. As PPKS celebrates its existence 27 years, we invite all pensioners in Sabah to join this movement. Membership is not just about personal benefits; it's about creating a stronger collective that can advocate for meaningful change. Together, we can ensure that all pensioner's golden years are filled with dignity, security, and purpose.Let us Honor the legacy of our service and work together to build a brighter future—one where pensioners are valued, cared for, and empowered to lead fulfilling lives.Join PPKS and be part of a community that truly understands your journey and works tirelessly to improve the lives of all pensioners. Together, we can make a difference. Let us all celebrate together the end of Covid 19 pandemic to all Sabahan

The Final Countdown of Invisible Adversity MCO lifted. Robert an executive banker, awoke to another dreary day within the confines of his home. There was nothing to look forward to, save for the numbing routine of being glued to the television or occasionally reading. His wife was constantly on her WhatsApp, engrossed in catching up with friends after months of Movement Control Order (MCO). She was so busy that she often missed their regular meals, opting for quick instant noodles instead. Robert spent his days in bed reading, knowing that nothing substantial awaited him. Out of the blue, his wife burst in, her excitement palpable. "The MCO has been lifted!" she shouted joyfully. "We can move around freely, go shopping, meet friends, and see our children!" The news breathed life into Robert. He jumped out of bed and immediately called his buddies to verify the declaration. By the afternoon, he was at their Favorite butterfly coffee shop in Donggonon Penampang hamlet, eagerly awaiting his friends. As they sipped their Favorite drinks, they chattered about everything under the sun, indulging in several cups of hot coffee. However, the gathering was cut short by the looming threat of rain clouds. They left the coffee shop immediately. Robert had to return fast to escape the oncoming storm, as the hamlet was prone to constant flooding. As he drove home, his mind turned despondent. He had heard that a good friend of his, a buddy he had known since childhood, had succumbed to health problems. Robert held this friend in high esteem for his social collaboration and involvement in many organizations and non-governmental activities. He was an outgoing man in the community, constantly helping others in need. Unfortunately, during the MCO, the restriction on his movements had taken a disturbing turn, disrupting his physical and emotional well-being. Gradually, stress took its toll, leading to a series of health issues. It became clear that he was a victim of Health activities. This unfortunate event stunned Robert to the core, filling him with a deep sense of sadness. Another friend of Robert had suffered dramatically after his compulsory third dose of the vaccine. Initially, he was in good spirits and even played a game of golf. But by the end of the Covid19 pandemic during a routine exercise, he had difficulty breathing rushed to the emergency ward. He spent several days in the ICU, but by the tenth day, he had succumbed to his illness. As a result of the MCO, Robert had lost several friends. He thanked God for His blessings that had kept his family safe. Life had to go on, he lamented, and now he was eager to reset his schedule and return to normalcy. Robert pondered how the virus had brought the world to its knees. Just as it had emerged suddenly, it was now gradually becoming a thing of the past, retreating to the shadows. The virus had spread its unrelenting wave of destruction, sparing no nation, including Malaysia. Fortunately, Malaysia's resilience had alleviated the ongoing calamity. Scientists and pharmaceutical companies worldwide were on high alert, using every available tool to find a remedy. Companies raced to develop a cure, knowing that a breakthrough would bring immense profits. The vaccine's effectiveness remained a contentious issue, with some medical professionals questioning its safety. Despite proven side effects, pharmaceutical companies often rebuffed these concerns with ambiguous explanations. Many people were sceptical, but government mandates left little room for opting out. It was clear that the cost of the vaccine was monumental, burdening financially weak economies. However, the Malaysian government managed to mitigate the issue, emerging relatively unscathed. For those who survived this episode, the long-term health effects remained uncertain. The COVID-19 storm was gradually dissipating, but the world had to remain vigilant for any future occurrences. The virus's origins and the criminal nature of its spread remained unresolved. As Malaysia lifted the MCO, a ray of hope emerged for a second rebirth. Factories, offices, businesses, and government departments resumed operations, bringing life back to the nation. Farmers could sell their goods, students returned to school, and families and friends could finally interact and socialize again. Robert felt a renewed sense of compassion and empathy for his fellow citizens. The moment had come for Malaysians to journey on the right path, fostering goodwill and reverting to normalcy. It's great to hear that activities by organizations that had been put on hold are gradually returning to normal. After disruptions like the pandemic or other challenges, it can be a significant relief to see things resuming.

PPKS activities resumed as normal

The Sabah Government Education Pensioners Association

The Sabah Government Education Pensioner Association began their activities in earnest to catch lost time. 5Ps" akin to Persatuan Pesara Pegawai Perkhidmatan Pendidikan they had endured adversity and tribulation of the highest order, but now they could breathe easier and reset their activities The window to the world was open once more, and life was returning to the way it once was.

Opportune time to hit the fairway by members of 5P after covid19 dilemma

In times of grief, families now find comfort in the opportunity to bid farewell to their loved ones, surrounded by relatives and friends who share in their sorrow. This sacred act of coming together to mourn and celebrate a life lost was a luxury denied to many during the harrowing days of the COVID-19 pandemic.

Back then, the strict restrictions imposed to curb the virus's spread meant that countless individuals passed away in isolation, cut off from the presence of their loved ones in their final moments. For many families, the grief was compounded by the inability to perform traditional rites or gather to honor the departed. Often, it was only the caregivers or healthcare workers who accompanied them to their graves, silent witnesses to an era marked by unimaginable loss.

The return to shared farewells today reminds us of the importance of connection, compassion, and closure in the journey of grief. It also serves as a stark reminder of the resilience and sacrifices made during a time when love could only be expressed from afar.

In their daily prayers, they remembered those whose lives had been taken abruptly, wishing them a safe journey to the realm of peace.

Second Episode

REFLECTIONS ON THE PAST

As we revisit these untold stories—from the abaca plantations to the Japanese occupation and the legends of Tinagat—we Honor the resilience, sacrifices, and spirit of those who came before us. These stories are not just history; they are threads that weave together the identity of Sabah, its people, and their connection to the land.

By sharing these memories, we ensure that the voices of the past are never forgotten. Through hardship and hope, the legacy of the abaca plantations, the occupation, the confrontation with Indonesia and the Tinagat tales' lives on, reminding us to cherish our heritage and preserve it for generations to come.

Peter Chin Sen Choo

Reminiscing BAL estate through the lens of Mr Peter Chin Peter Chin Sen Choo Peter was born, and lived his entire life in a quaint village nestled within the vast expanse of the Abaca Plantation in Tawau Hamlet. The village, shrouded in the shadows of towering hemp and rubber trees, was a place of both struggle and inspiration for Peter. As a child, Peter witnessed the relentless toil of his parents, labouring day and night in the hemp and rubber factories.

Workers at the hemp factory in BAL estate

The Abaca Hemp factory The Hemp factory in BAL estate Their sweat and perseverance were etched into the very fabric of his upbringing. These hardships became the bedrock of Peter's determination to forge a brighter future for himself and his family. Even as a young boy, Peter was known for his wit and curiosity. The wilderness around him served as his playground, a boundless realm of adventure and discovery. He and his gang of friends roamed the lush, untamed bush, their laughter echoing through the trees.

The clear crystal stream

The crystal-clear, unpolluted streams that meandered through the village were a constant source of delight, where they would catch the ferocious feeding frenzy of the silver carps. Every few minutes, their fishing lines would pull up a prized catch, carps the size of three fingers—a good outing by any measure. Terrapins turtle thrived on the water spinach (kangkong) that flourished by the riverbanks. Giant, mature terrapins could weigh up to three kilograms or more, though the later widespread use of pesticides and weed killers decimated their numbers Bombalai, the village in the north of Tawau, was a place of rustic charm. The old, dilapidated wooden buildings left by the Japanese plantation company had been repaired and refurbished by the new administration.

The British company, eager to revive the economy of Tawau Residency, further developed the plantation industry, building more housing for the executives and repairing old Japanese accommodations for the expanded workforce. Spacious buildings were converted into temporary schools or accommodations for cadets and officers. The dark secret of the buildings occupied by the Japanese remained hidden until the late Tsurumi Yoshiyuki, a renowned Japanese research scholar on agriculture and aquaculture, visited the place in 1993. Walking through the overgrown paths, Tsurumi rekindled about the dark days when his dead officer friends were laid in rows in those rooms. With trembling hands, he calmly took photos of the compound and buildings, preserving memories that would haunt him until his last days. During the Japanese reign under the Kuhara Estate Company

Mr Kuhara Fusanoskauke founder Kuhara Estate administration,

Table Estate served as their headquarters. It was a hub of activity with HQ offices, estate offices, an old clubhouse, VIP quarters for the Japanese, a mortuary, a hemp factory, and more. In the late 50s, as BAL expanded, more staff were recruited and the cadet training program was introduced. As the family population increased more children of schooling age required education. Vernacular Chinese schools already existed in major estates like Table, Merotai, and Imam, established by local Chinese communities.

Locomotive to ferry goods to the jetty

Bombalai, initially a minor administration center with a good jetty to ship out bales of hemp and a central workshop, had no plantation. Locomotive to transport company produce

The rubber factory in BAL estate

The pioneers of Chinese education in gudang 4 at BAL estgate

The Chinese primary school where Peter studied Courtesy of Workers sent their children to these vernacular schools, with many students coming from Gudang 4, where Peter studied for two years.

The Chinese school Peter studied for two years

The company was obligated to send staff children to English schools in town on company transport, mostly British Land Rovers. The author who studied in Holy Trinity school at that time used to witness the BAL children alighting from their vehicle However, as the number of staff children increased, it became costly and cumbersome due to the long, bumpy, and dusty roads. To alleviate this, the company amalgamated all vernacular schools and started the Abaca Primary School, English medium, at Table Estate in 1960. Elder Chinese folks who had worked for Kuhara Estate Co. as coolies and survived WWII recounted tales of skirmishes between Allied Forces and the Japanese army during the Second World War of 1945. Important high-ranking Japanese soldiers who perished in these battles were not left behind or buried in the plantations.

Old building utilised by the Japanese as temporary mortuary for Japanese official who died during classes in the estate during the end of the second world war in 1945

Their corpses were secretly brought to a small house, preserved while awaiting transport back to Japan for honourable burials. The building used by the Japanese as temporary mortuary This house, now used for various functions by cadets, teachers, and personnel, had once served as a WWII temporary mortuary for VIP Japanese soldiers. Close to the building was the cadet mess, a stone's throw from Peter's class. He often witnessed the energetic cadets congregating there for their morning break, the roaring sound of their bikes occasionally interrupting his class. The young girls would watch, captivated by the cadets' tales and the allure of potential On weekends, the cadets mingled with the expatriates The BAL executive Club romance. at the exclusive BAL Executive Club, watching Cowboy and Tarzan films premiered before they were screened free for workers the following week at the open Padang.

The BAL executive Club House

As a young lad, Peter would eagerly request more than one helping of the free Ovaltine drinks given to the children. Little did he know that twenty years later, while working for Harrisons and Crosfield, he would be the one distributing free Milo drinks for 22 years, a role he once enjoyed so much. The cadets played a pioneering role in promoting planting as a profession among the young people of Tawau. The author personally met several of them at the executive clubs and occasionally met the senior manager of BAL, Mr. Jack Bridger at the Tawau Sports Club situated by the Seaside Tawau town. Mr. Bridger, formerly a military officer who took part in the Japanese surrender in North Borneo, joined the British company in BAL after resigning his commission. It was his no-nonsense management ability that disciplined the cadets during their training sessions in BAL. Married to a beautiful Indonesian woman, he had several children. The author had the privilege of meeting him while he was attached to a local company in Tawau after his retirement from BAL. Another BAL socially executive that I often met was Mr John Raddy A keen darter who encouraged me on the games of dart during social encounters at the Tawau Sports Club.

Tawau was renowned for its fertile land, especially the Tiger area with its volcanic soil. There was a saying that if you stuck a walking cane into the soil, it would grow. Several cadets, such as Edward Chong, Titus Ng, Ricky Chin, Richard Mok, Albert Chong, and Anthony Tsen, came from Holy Trinity School. Albert, a hero in BAL field events, outperformed sturdy plantation workers in the annual BAL Sports Meet. Jaswant Singh Kler, another cadet, excelled in track events and later became a manager like Mr. Thong and Mr. Dickson Chok from the pioneer cadet batch. During the Kuhara Estate Co. and later BAL era, many historical buildings were demolished, erasing the tales of the Japanese in Tawau. The British BAL constructed a new HQ at Bombalai in 1958/59, and the vacated buildings were converted into the Abaca Primary (English) School, revamping the estate's education system. The company had an obligation to provide basic facilities such as schools, electricity, water, and welfare to employees. This policy led to the establishment of the Abaca Primary School, English medium, at Table Estate, catering to the staff's children and saving costs. When Golden Hope took over the plantation, many wooden buildings built by the Japanese were demolished, erasing the historical iconic structures and the tales of the Japanese presence in the Tawau hamlet. Several cadets who climbed the ladder found their life partners among the BAL beauties and now live happily as planters' wives in Tawau. Many of the existing cadets still reunite intermittently, except for those who have passed away. 'As the story goes, many cadets found their significant others among the BAL beauties. These cadets, well-acquainted with the local community, included Albert Chong, Leslie, Austin Kuchi, Thomas Baran Dickson Chok, Jaswant Singh, Enrique Salazar, Anthony Tsen, David Lim, and a few others. In the end, Peter's story is one of resilience, community, and the relentless pursuit of a better future. His journey from a small village in Abaca Plantation to becoming a respected figure in education is a testament to the power of hard work and determination. The legacy of the depths and the rich history of the plantation continues to be a source of inspiration for generations to come, especially to the young youth of Tawau Rekindle their journey from the past.

Third Episode

Austin Bugat after retirement The destiny of a Planter in BAL estate from Sarawak

In the heart of Sebubu, a quaint village along the Mapar River, the air was alive with the symphony of the jungle. It was 1944, and the arrival of a newborn baby in the home of Mr. Bugat anak Semen, the respected Tuai Rumah, (Headman) was cause for celebration. Mr. Bugat, a subsistence farmer who grew both hill and swamp rice, returned from the river with a bountiful catch, his heart full of gratitude. As he approached his home, he was greeted by a joyful commotion; his wife had just given birth to a son, Austin Bugat. The newborn's cries blend harmoniously with the jungle's melody, signalling a new chapter in the family's life. Despite the joy, the backdrop of World War II cast a shadow over the village. Sarawak, under Japanese occupation since 1943, was a place of tension and vigilance. Mr. Bugat's journey to town for supplies and to register his son's birth was fraught with danger. Japanese soldiers, stationed at every strategic corner, monitor the area with suspicion. The converted Kuching prison now holds war prisoners, and fear pervades the air. Mr. Bugat navigated this perilous environment carefully, aware that many had been arrested on flimsy charges. Back in Sebubu, Mr. Bugat shared his concerns about Japanese expansion with the community, urging them to prepare and conserve resources. The village, surrounded by natural defences like dense forests and rugged terrain, remained relatively safe from Japanese incursion. Weekly gatherings in the longhouse see elders recounting tales of Sarawak's head-hunter past and discussing pressing issues, like the difficulties of education in such remote areas. For young Austin, life in the village was both a blend of tradition and challenge. Education was a struggle, with the dangerous jungle paths, wildlife encounters, and seasonal floods making school attendance odious. Despite these obstacles, Austin's early years were shaped by tribal customs and a deep connection to his heritage. The stories of Raja Brooke and the headhunting era, though fading, still hold sway over the imagination of the village's youth. As Austin grew older, the pursuit of education became even more challenging. Secondary school required traveling 80 kilometres on foot on the treacherous paths for two whole days to reach the Anglican St Augustine Secondary School, where he boarded for three years. His academic journey was fraught with interruptions due to the harsh realities of life in Sarawak. Despite his sporadic schooling and a setback in his junior high results, Austin persevered. He secured a temporary teaching position to assist his family income and an opportunity to prepare for his exams as a private candidate and ultimately succeeded.

Austin in Kuching in 1963

He was recommended to continue his studies in Kuching to archive his dream. Due to financial constrained he had to accept the reality of life and opted to dive into the workforce. After a search he finally found a prospect of entering into a training program in the agriculture field as a cadet in the agriculture sector in Johor and was admitted to pursue a three-year course of Cadetship under the same company as BAL. Called Kulai Oil Palm Estate. a subsidiary of the Commonwealth Development Corporation. After graduating from his three years cadetship and worked for several months on the job plantation, Austin's career took a pivotal turn when he was transferred to BAL Tawau in 1965, a plantation managed by the Commonwealth Development Corporation. The arrival at BAL was a revelation; to see the vast expanses of Manila abaca plants similar to banana plants was a sharp contrast to the oil palm plantations he previously knew. The estate's former Japanese wooden house, formerly used as a temporary mortuary now his temporary accommodation, initially seems daunting, but Austin adopted quickly, drawing on his past experiences. At BAL Tawau, Austin navigated the challenges of managing a diverse workforce and adapting to the new environment. His leadership skills were honed through a rigorous training program at the Outward-Bound School in Lumut, Perak. Over his 25 years at

BAL, Austin proved himself to be a diligent, personable, and effective planter. His professional journey was marked by both triumphs and trials, including his eventual marriage to a local Tawau woman in 1970.Upon retiring from BAL in 1989, Austin transitions to working with the Sarawak Agency Salcra. At 80, he finally stepped away from his professional life, ready to embrace a new chapter of travel and exploration. His retirement, marked by a sense of fulfillment and nostalgia, reflects a life well-lived—one shaped by the rhythms of the jungle, the trials of wartime, and the enduring spirit of resilience.

Reunion of BAL Ex- personal and their spouse has been most welcome to rekindle their bygone days in BAL estate, Tawau, Sabah.

Footnote

Transformation of Borneo Abaca Plantation

1. *KUHARA ESTATER COMPANY 1916-1949 29,325 ACRBES GRANTED TO KUHARA TO PLANT RUBBER AN MANILA HEMP 2) BORNEO ABACA LIMITED 1949-2006 3)GOLDEN HOPE 1996-2007 4) 2007 SIME DARBY PLANTATION BHD 5) April 2024 proposed name changed to SD Gutherie bhd*

Fourth Episode

THE JAPANESE OCCUPATION OF NORTH BORNEO

The Japanese Atrocity in North Borneo is well documented

Peter Raymond Lai Kui Fook KM

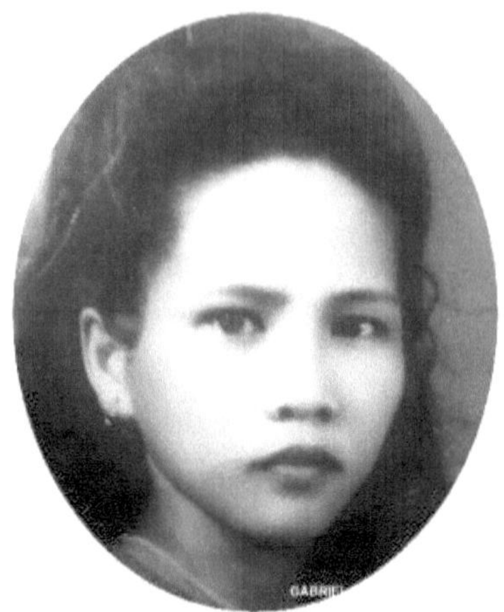

Gabriela Remedia Villalobos
Born in Sandakan on the 18th
March 1926

Courage in the Cause of Freedom Peter Raymond Lai Kui Fook

Peter Raymond Lai Kui Fook A Legacy of Courage and compassion, Peter Raymond Lai Kui Fook, born on July 1, 1925, in Papar, North Borneo (now Sabah), was the third son of Augustine Lai Man and Magdalena Yap Nyuk Lan a Sino Bisaya/Kadazan of Beaufort. His early life was marked by both personal tragedy and resilience. At the tender age of six, Peter faced the loss of his mother, who passed away after giving birth to his sister, Theresa. The responsibility of raising Peter and his siblings—Joseph, Simon, Paul, and Theresa—fell upon their elderly and ailing grandmother, Mary Lim. Realizing the challenges ahead, Peter's uncle, Lai Pan, took the decisive step of relocating the children to Sandakan, where they were entrusted to the care of the Catholic Mission at St Marys church and convent". Peter and his brothers were placed in St. Mary's Boarding House, while Theresa was taken in by St. Mary's Convent. These institutions not only provided them with shelter and education but also instilled in them values of self-reliance, faith, and compassion. The boys attended St. Mary's Secondary School, where they developed a strong foundation in both academics and moral values. At seventeen, Peter completed his schooling as World War 11 looming over the horizon. He quickly secured a position as a dresser at the Sandakan Civil Hospital in 1942. His proficiency in English, coupled with his intelligence and compassionate nature, made him an invaluable asset to the hospital. His natural aptitude for caring for the sick and wounded, earned him the admiration of his superiors. It was during this time that Peter met Gabriela Remedia Lobos, a spirited and beautiful woman of Filipino and Spanish descent. Despite initial resistance from Peters families, their love prevailed, and they were united in marriage—a testament to their unwavering commitment to each other.

World War II and the Japanese Invasion of North Borneo The peace and stability in Peter's life were shattered by the outbreak of World War II and the subsequent Japanese invasion of Borneo. Despite the challenges and dangers that lay ahead, Peter's courage and dedication to his family and community remained steadfast. Meanwhile in Sandakan, the Japanese military erected a formidable, walled compound designed to house prisoners of war from Singapore. Inside, the conditions were dire. The Australian and British captives faced brutal treatment, compounded by a severe lack of medical care. With no access to essential drugs, their suffering was profound. Dr. Taylor, the civil service medical officer stationed in Sandakan, found himself grappling with a moral quandary. Despite the immense danger, he resolved to secretly supply the prisoners with crucial medical supplies. Peter and his small band of accomplices were tasked with this perilous mission. For months, they expertly navigated the dangers of their covert operation, managing to deliver the life-saving supplies under the radar of the ever-watchful Japanese authorities. The operation was fraught with tension, but their stealth and determination kept the prisoners' spirits and health from deteriorating further. However, their luck ran out in July 1943, just a month after Bryan's birth. The Japanese military police launched a violent raid on Peter's home. The door was shattered as armed soldiers stormed in, dragging Peter from his wife's embrace. He was unceremoniously thrown into a truck, his screams echoing in the night as they sped towards Tanah Merah. The next day Gabriella father Mr A.V. Lobos

A.V. Lobos

Gabriella and a Japanese friend went to see the prison security officer. Their request to meet Peter was denied. Gabriella had no choice but to stay with her parents' family at Kampong Gulam. There, the prisoners of war awaited their transfer to the Japanese court in Kuching, their fate hanging precariously in the balance. Among the arrested was Gabriela's sister Tasiana's husband, Felix Azcona, who had been accused covertly aiding the Allied forces. His role in the underground operation made him a marked man. A few months later, both Peter and Azcona were transported to Kuching. At the Japanese court, Peter was condemned to 20 years of hard labor, while Azcona was sentenced to death. When the war ended in 1945, the Australian military liberated the prisoners, offering them a long-awaited reprieve. Yet, the shadow of betrayal soon fell over their efforts. The operation's secret was exposed, not by the enemy, but by a disgruntled insider. One of the wives of the covert members, dissatisfied with her share of the supplies, revealed their clandestine activities to the Japanese authorities. Her betrayal brought a tragic end to their noble but perilous Endeavor, casting a somber light on their courageous acts of defiance.

BACK TO SANDAKAN:

The Return of Peter Lai In the waning months of 1945, the war had finally loosened its grip on Southeast Asia. Peter Lai, adorned in his military uniform and armed with a rifle, descended from a small aircraft onto the familiar yet profoundly changed landscape of Sandakan Jetty. Among those waiting anxiously was Gabriela, his devoted wife and her sister Tasina., her heart racing with anticipation as she scanned the crowd for a glimpse of her husband. The war had kept them apart, and now, after years of uncertainty and fear, they were to be reunited. As Peter made his way down from the Sunderland plane and disembark from the jetty, he caught sight of his family, but the reunion was not without its bittersweet moments. Little Bryan, who had grown in his father's absence, looked at the man in uniform with trepidation. When Peter knelt to embrace him, Bryan recoiled, tears streaming down his face. The boy did not recognize the man who had left them so long ago, the man who had survived the horrors of war. It took time and patience for Peter to reconnect with his son, but gradually, the bond between father and child was restored, and the family began to heal.. Returning to civilian life, Peter was reappointed to his former position at a local clinic at Mile 8, where he had served before the war. His skills as a dresser were soon called upon once more, but this time he was called upon to serve in the Kinabatangan district, the wildest region of Borneo.

*Peter in Tongod Kinabatangan Hamlet No 1 Doctor from Sandakan
No 2 Simon Lai No 3 Peter Raymond La no 4 the author Bryan No 5
shopkeeper No 6 Datuk Malik Chua's father*

They had to travel by boat through the Kinabatangan River in
Tongod prefecture. Peter served in Tongod for a year before his work
would be recognized in a way that few could have imagined.

Not long after his return, Peter received word from the medical officer that he was to be awarded the King's Medal, a prestigious Honor bestowed by the Australian and British Commonwealth of Nations. The award recipients Peter receiving the award Peter in Jesselton

Award recipient welcomed by the British Consulate

Peter receiving his award (KM)

This recognition was not just for his service during the war, but for the extraordinary courage he had shown in the face of unspeakable adversity. The award ceremony took place on January 21, 1947, a date that would forever be etched in Peter's memory. The Governor of North Borneo presented the medal in Jesselton, marking the occasion as one of both solemnity and Honor. As Peter accepted the medal, his thoughts were not of himself, but of his comrades—those brave souls who had participate alongside him, many of whom had paid the ultimate price. He thought of those who had been beheaded or executed, their lives cut short by the brutality of war. With the weight of the medal in his hand, Peter prayed silently that their sacrifices would never be forgotten, that their legacy would endure in the memories of those who lived on.

From left: The author Bryan Paul Lai, Peter Raymond Lai, Daniel Lai, Gabriella Remedia Lobos and Cabrini Rosemary Lai in Jesselton North Borneo in 1948

After the ceremony, Peter settled in Jesselton for some time in the civil hospital before being transferred once more to the Lahad Datu district civil hospital. A year later in 1950 Peter left the government service into a quieter life at Wallace Bay on Sebatik Island, where he took up a position as the chief dresser in charge of the dispensary for the Bombay Burma Trading Corporation.

Peters' family in Wallace Bay, Sebatik island

Lais family in Wallace Bay Sebatik Island Though the war was over, its impact on Peter was profound. The once sociable man now found solace in solitude, the shadows of the past lingering in his mind. He became more reserved, wary of those around him, and often questioned who among his acquaintances could have betrayed the group during those dark times.

Fifth Episode

RISKING ALL FOR DUTY

Mr Patrick Valutanan Lingham MBE

Puan Theresa Majair

Spouse of Patrick Lingham

During the Second World War, from 1941 to 1945, a tranquil village nestled amidst the breathtaking tapestry of mountain ranges and dense rainforests stood as a testament to centuries of indigenous life. This remote hamlet, vastly unpopulated, was home to nomadic tribes whose existence was intricately linked to the jungle that surrounded them. Clad in traditional loincloths (cawat), these resilient people roamed the verdant undergrowth, relying on their skills to hunt for sustenance. Their blowpipes, the weapon of choice, were a symbol of their deep connection to the land and its resources. Over time, some tribes sought the safety of longhouses, built for mutual protection against intruders. Those who dared to infiltrate their territory faced swift and brutal consequences, often meeting their end through the traditional practice of beheading. However, as the community evolved and the realities of life changed, such violent practices gradually faded, giving way to a more harmonious existence among the tribes. With the arrival of early Asian migrants, brought in by English enterprises, the formerly quiet village began to transform into a bustling town. These newcomers opened small businesses, infusing the area with fresh energy and opportunity. The once mundane village blossomed, welcoming the establishment of essential administrative services, including hospitals and missionary schools, which further integrated the local population into a broader socio-economic landscape. Yet, this burgeoning progress was soon overshadowed by the darkness of war. The idyllic life of the villagers was shattered as the Japanese forces invaded, bringing with them a wave of terror and brutality that would forever alter the fabric of North Borneo. As a result of the historical transformations, several towns in North Borneo has blossomed into a beautiful, peaceful, and well-established administrative center, gracefully nestled between winding rivers and undulating hills. The town of Tenom serves as the final railway link running from Jesselton, connecting several towns along its scenic route. The railway, a significant achievement of the British Chartered Company, played a crucial role in shaping the early history of North Borneo. Once a mundane agricultural settlement, Tenom has evolved dramatically over the years, thanks to the hard work of British colonialists and various migrant laborers who toiled in the lush plantations that surround the area. Among these migrant groups was the father of Mr. Patrick Lingham, who settled in Papar. Hailing from Ceylon, Mr Ananda Lingham was brought in by the British to assist in the operation of the only railway in North Borneo. Assigned to the small town of Papar, he gradually integrated into the local community, earning the affectionate nickname Tambi. Though his real name was Ananda Lingham, he became a beloved figure in the area, known for his warm demeanour and dedication to his work. Over time, he established deep connections with the locals, symbolizing the blending of cultures and the shared history that characterizes this region. With its rich tapestry of history and community, Papar stands today as a testament to resilience and growth, a place where the echoes of the past harmoniously intertwine with the vibrant life of its present inhabitants. With his mindful and friendly character, Ananda quickly caught the attention of a beautiful young Bruneian woman named Salmah Tahir Their love blossomed effortlessly, transcending the boundaries of race and culture. After some time spent getting to know each other, Ananda mustered the courage to declare his feelings, and they soon married. A year later, they welcomed a son Patrick into the world, further binding their families together. Growing up within this vibrant community, Patrick received his education locally and immersed himself in the rich cultural tapestry that surrounded him. His warm demeanour and genuine interest in others mirrored his father's character, allowing him to forge strong bonds with the townspeople. It wasn't long before he caught the eye of a local woman, Theresa Majair. Their love was intense and passionate, and they ultimately tied the knot, celebrating their union amidst the supportive embrace of their friends and family in Papar. Following their marriage, Patrick was assigned to several districts by the Charted company as a telephone operator, gaining invaluable experience that would shape his career. His journey eventually led him to Tenom, a town brimming with promise and opportunity. Known for its diverse population, Tenom was a place where various races lived side by side in peaceful harmony, all striving for a better life. Patrick's dedication and hard work did not go unnoticed. As he consistently fulfilled his duties with unwavering commitment, he steadily climbed the ranks within the department, earning promotions that reflected his efforts and integrity. His journey was not just a personal success but also a testament to the community's spirit, as they all thrived together in the pursuit of prosperity and unity. Patrick's family had settled comfortably in Tenom, eagerly anticipating a promising future. As the months unfolded, his wife, Theresa, was filled with excitement, awaiting the arrival of their new baby. Unbeknownst to them, the world beyond their tranquil home was spiralling into chaos. In the West, human greed and power-hungry leaders were driving nations toward conflict, while in the East, Japan was poised to annex its Asian neighbors in a ruthless bid for imperial dominance. Rational thought and moral empathy seemed to vanish amidst the rising tide of hostility. Despite the brewing storm of animosity just beyond their borders, Patrick remained focused on what truly mattered to him—his family and the new life soon to join them. As the war ignited in Europe in 1939, their son, Wilfred, was born, bringing an overwhelming sense of joy to both Patrick and Theresa. They welcomed their healthy child with open arms, their hearts brimming with love and hope for the future. However, as the sun rose on a new year in 1941, the warlike Japanese imperial army began its planned invasion, casting a dark shadow over their peaceful existence. Despite the impending turmoil, Patrick and Theresa continued to dream of a blissful life together, cherishing their growing family and the simple moments of joy that filled their days. Patrick continued to work tirelessly, dedicated to providing the Tenom community with the latest communication services. He was aware of the Japanese advance throughout the Asian region, yet he maintained his focus on his daily responsibilities, striving to keep the lines of communication open. The rumblings of war were growing louder, with the Japanese war machine sweeping across the continent, inching closer to their doorstep. Military garrisons began to emerge in towns like Jesselton, Sandakan, Tawau, and other small communities, casting a shadow of anxiety over the land. Despite the mounting tension, Patrick pressed on with his duties in the department, though a sense of unease settled within him. He understood that the Japanese would soon take over the administration of the town, but he was determined to fulfill his role, even as interruptions by Japanese military personnel became increasingly common. Unbeknownst to him, his name had been shortlisted by the occupying forces, placing him in grave danger. The telecom department, the only one capable of facilitating communication around the world, became a target of interest for the Japanese. One fateful night, Patrick's blissful life was shattered when a group of Japanese kampitai violently burst into his home. Patrick and his family were soundly asleep when the horrifying events unfolded. Suddenly, the deafening crash of the front door being kicked in jolted them awake, sending terror rippling through their hearts. Theresa, who had been sleeping beside their child, shot upright at the sound. Heart racing, she rushed toward the living room, her mind racing with dread, thinking that a tropical storm has hit the house. As she stepped into the dimly lit space, her worst fears materialized before her eyes: the door lay in ruins, and a group of armed kampitai stormed in, pushing her aside with ruthless disregard. They shouted for Patrick to come out, their voices echoing with menace. Still clad in his pyjamas, Patrick instinctively emerged, ready to reason with the intruders. But before he could utter a word, one of the soldiers struck him brutally across the head with the butt of a rifle. The force of the blow sent Patrick crashing to the ground, his world spinning into darkness as pain and confusion engulfed humified, roused by the terrifying commotion, stumbled into the living room, his heart racing. The sight that met his innocent eyes was one of pure horror: his father, Patrick, sprawled on the floor, writhing in pain. The air was thick with fear as Wilfred's small frame trembled, unable to comprehend the violence unfolding before him. Panic surged through him, and he let out a desperate cry, reaching for his mother, seeking solace in her presence. His elder sister, jolted awake by the chaos, sat frozen in shock, her wide eyes reflecting the terror of the moment. Overwhelmed, she instinctively crawled beneath the bed, shivering as she clutched her knees, trying to block out the nightmare that invaded their home. Meanwhile, Wilfred clung tightly to his mother, his small hands gripping her arm like a lifeline. As he raised his head, he caught sight of the soldiers—cold, ruthless figures—dragging his father across the floor, showing no hint of compassion. Tears streamed down his cheeks as he watched in horror, his heart shattering at the sight of his father's agony. The kampitai, with their hard faces and steely determination, roughly hoisted Patrick, ignoring his cries of pain as they dragged him toward their waiting military vehicle. This was the last time Theresa and her son would see Patrick. As the soldiers forced him out into the night, disappearing into the shadows, Wilfred felt an icy grip of terror wrap around his heart. He buried his face in his mother's side, sobbing uncontrollably, unable to process the brutality of what had just happened. The night air was cool, but his body felt like it was on fire with fear, a chilling reminder of the cruelty they had just witnessed. Theresa, holding her son tightly, felt her heart ache as she stared into the dark void where her husband had vanished. In that moment, she realized that their lives would never be the same again, marked forever by the violent hand of war. Wilfred continued to cry, his innocent mind grappling with the unimaginable horror of the night, haunted by the cruel fate that had befallen his father. As Patrick lay on the fringe of the forest lifeless, three Muruts hunters saw the whole episode and waited for the Japanese to leave before bringing Patrick to their village for treatment. Muruts set to work, expertly crafting remedies from the rich flora around them. They applied poultices and brewed potent teas, working tirelessly to stabilize him and bring him back from the brink of death. Meanwhile, Theresa had returned to Papar with her children, her heart heavy with despair. She struggled with the overwhelming fear that she might never see her beloved husband again. The uncertainty gnawed at her soul, yet amidst the darkness, a flicker of hope remained. Deep within her, she clung to the belief that a miracle could still happen, and she turned to prayer, imploring for her husband's survival and for the strength to face the days ahead without him. Living in constant fear, Theresa's heart shattered like a thousand pieces of glass, each fragment representing the hope and joy that had been ripped away from her life. Yet, amidst the pain, she found solace among her family clan, their presence a fragile balm for her wounded spirit. Years slipped by in a blur, The end of the war and the return of Patrick V. Lingham By 1945, the war was beginning to wind down. On August 15, 1945, the news of Japan's surrender swept through the land, casting a newfound light over the darkness that had enveloped them for so long. Now six years old, Wilfred stood at the window, his small figure framed by the fading sunlight as he gazed out, longing for his father. The questions spilled from his lips, innocent and desperate: "Where is Dad?" Each inquiry pierced Theresa's heart anew, and all she could do was hold him tight, tears streaming down her cheeks, mourning the father Wilfred barely knew. At night, Wilfred was haunted by dreams of that fateful day when his father had been taken, the memories swirling in his mind like ghosts, leaving him bewildered and scared. Theresa, too, found herself caught in the web of dreams, visions of Patrick returning home, holding her and their children close. Each morning, she awoke in a haze, her heart aching as she watched Wilfred and his sister sleeping soundly beside her, blissfully unaware of the turmoil that had torn their family apart. One day, while gathering bamboo shoots in the jungle, Theresa's ears caught the distant cries of her friends. Her heart raced as panic surged through her; could it be? The news seemed too unbelievable to grasp, and she stood frozen, questioning whether it was another cruel false alarm. "Is this a dream?" she lamented, her pulse pounding in her ears. When she finally reached home, she sat down, her hands trembling as she listened to the narrative once more, desperate to confirm that this wasn't just another figment of her imagination. As the reality sank in—Patrick was alive, recuperating from the horrifying torture he had endured and brought to a village called Kampong Kinabong—joy exploded within her like fireworks in the night sky. Wilfred and his sister, who had been playing nearby, rushed over, their faces lighting up with uncontainable excitement as they heard the news. Their laughter filled the air, a sweet melody of hope and reunion. But there was still a journey ahead. Theresa and her family clan had to travel far to reach Kampong Kinabong, needing permission from the authorities to ensure the Japanese military had disarmed and that the area was under the control of the Allied forces. As soon as the coast was clear, the following day, Theresa and her relatives set out for Kampong Kinabong, hearts racing with anticipation, their spirits buoyed by the prospect of reuniting with Patrick. Each step felt lighter as they moved closer to their beloved, each heartbeat a reminder that hope had not abandoned them after all. Patrick was reinstated in his old job and later promoted as the director of Telecom He was awarded the MBE by the British government. Due to the injuries, he received during the war he died at the age of 57

Sixth Episodes

THE TINAGAT LEGACY

BEACH IN TAWAU

The Tinagat Beach in Tawau Nestled beside the rugged hills of Tawau in North Borneo, Tinagat Beach might f irst appear as a mere strip of rocky coast, hiding quietly within the charming confines of Tawau. A journey down the narrow, pebble-dotted path of Apas Road leads to what seems like an ordinary beach. But for me, Tinagat Beach hums with a deep, personal resonance. It's far more than a strip of sand; it's a vault of precious memories, a haven of my youth where I sought peace and renewal. This special retreat has guided me a plethora of happy memories, now kindling warmth in my heart and coaxing smiles in my later years, reminiscent of the unwavering presence of an old, trusted companion. Tinagat stands as the only sandy retreat for the Tawau community, doubling as a blissful escape and a recreational haven for those escaping the grind of daily life. The beach, with its silver sands, and the almost mystical breeze promising to carry away grief and lighten burdened spirits, is a magical place. The gentle waves occasionally bestow the shore with rascally shaped driftwood, each a coveted treasure for the beach comers. I too have gathered an adored assembly of these sea sculpted artworks, now proudly displayed in my home, every piece narrated its unique tale. Among my earliest memories of this cherished beach is a recollection from 1957, when at fourteen, I was invited to the home of a close friend whose family was once attached to the Balit Estate in Kinabatangan prefecture

After the second world war in 1945, the family moved to Tawau and built a house at Apas Road mile three.

The family clan of Mr Ku Chen Yin William COURTESY OF Mr James Ku

His family's house, a quaint wooden structure, nestled within a verdant coconut grove, captured the spirit of those carefree, youthful days – memories that remain vividly imprinted in my mind, forever intertwined with the tranquil allure of Tinagat Beach. From my initial visit, I was embraced with warm hospitality by the family. Thereafter, Thomas' house became my monthly sanctuary, a world away from the chaotic life at the boarding house at Holy Trinity Catholic School. During those visits, Thomas and I often found ourselves unwinding at a nearby beach, a mere short walk from the house or on occasion's searching for squirrels hiding on the coconut canopies. Thomas is good at his homemade catapult. The little beast no matter how smart it was, could not escape and many fell prey to Thomas expertise.

One particular day, as we relaxed on an old log by the shore, a stone throw from his house, sharing stories and laughter everything under the sun. Thomas proposed a bicycle outing to another beach and then on to Apas Parit.

From left: Thomas Ku, Paul Jaikul, Paul Ku, Martin Liang, Jullie Ku
and Joseph Ku

I listened, intrigued by his plan but sceptical about the long ride, having never travelled such distances or explored unknown terrains before. Walking along the beach, Thomas detailed the location; trying to persuade me that the bike ride would be an exciting, trouble-free adventure. I was hesitant at first, up until he revealed passing through Tinagat Beach. The indication of Tinagat sparked a flood of memories. I was instantly transported back in time. I was with several other boys sitting on a small log by the Tawau river side close to a small hut formerly Rev father Ma was staying fishing for small fish before embarking on our search for young coconut to supplement our nutrition need. Out of the blue, Father Bekama came out and instructed me to meet him immediately. That call made me apprehension and wonders what fault have I done. It's not usual for the rector to call any boys on Saturday morning. Rev Father Bekama Promptly I responded, only to be told to be ready with few of my belonging. I followed him to his car and off we went to icebox on his speed boat. Our first destination was in Sebatik island to my home town. A taste of mom's food in the offing. After the mass at the Sebatik chapel, we proceed to Kalabakan river.

The Kalabakan River

That was in 1957 A trip that till today still lingers in my mind the precarious position we were in, when Rev Father Bekama and I found ourselves unexpectedly stranded on that very beach, shadowed by a lighthouse. As evening descended upon Kalabakan village, the day's duties were coming to an end for Rev Father Bekama. We had just concluded the mass at the chapel, where I served as his altar boy. The villagers, ever concerned and hospitable, urged Father Bekama to stay overnight, fearing for our safety due to the looming bad weather. The Kalabakan River, known for its sudden, dangerous swells in the flood season, posed a real threat. Its waters, teeming with crocodiles and riddled with debris, had been the downfall of many small boats. Despite their pleas, Father Bekama was resolute in his decision to leave. An important engagement awaited him the following day in Tawau, and we couldn't afford any delays. Ignoring their well-intentioned advice, we embarked on our journey from the jetty that very evening. As we meandered down the river, the serene sight of crocodiles and monkeys lounging along the banks belied the danger that lay ahead. About an hour later, we reached the river's estuary and ventured into the open sea. Here, Father Bekama, exhausted from the day's exertions, handed me the responsibility of steering our boat and quickly succumbed to a deep slumber. Navigating vigilantly towards Tawau, the faint outlines of the town were a reassuring sign. But nature had other plans. Suddenly, a formidable dark cloud loomed above us, heralding strong winds and ominous weather. The sea grew tumultuous, the boat pitching wildly with the waves. Dusk was turning into a fearsome night, with howling winds and lightning tearing across the sky, followed by torrential rain. Throughout this maelstrom, Rev.Father Bekama remained in a deep, undisturbed sleep, seemingly oblivious to the peril that surrounded us. I gripped the helm, fighting fatigue and cold, my eyes desperately searching for any hint of light from Tawau. But visibility was poor, the outlines of our destination blurred and distant. Fear crept in as the severity of our situation dawned on me. The thought of being lost at sea, never to see my family or love ones again, filled me with dread. The vast, unyielding ocean seemed ready to swallow us whole, erasing our existence. But in the heart of that storm, with desperation and determination battling within me, I held onto the helm, steering us through the unforgiving night, hoping against all odds to find our way back to safety. Miraculously, our little boat held strong against the relentless onslaught of the punishing waves. Realizing the gravity of our predicament, I knew it was time for Father Bekama to take the helm. But before I could rouse him, a monstrous wave crashed into us, nearly sending him overboard. This abrupt danger snapped him out of his slumber. With remarkable agility and presence of mind, he steadied himself and took control of the boat. Even now, I marvel at how Father Bekama remained unflappable and focused amidst the chaos, while I trembled, drenched and petrified. My prayers for deliverance rose fervently, a plea for guidance through the tempest. Perhaps it was divine intervention, as the storm gradually began to weaken. The rain eased, but the sea remained a churning mass, with the wind moaning a ghostly tune. We navigated blindly through the darkness, unsure of our direction, until suddenly, a faint glimmer of light pierced the night sky. Initially we were uncertain, my heart leapt when the light flashed again. Father Bekama, too, notched it and steered our course towards this beacon of hope.

The Tawau light house situated on a hill at Tinagat

The Tinagat light house Following this guiding light, we eventually made landfall, miraculously finding refuge on a beach. I whispered prayers of gratitude, overwhelmed by the mercy shown to us. The ordeal at the Cowie Harbour wasn't over yet. We had to spend the night in our boat, now safe from the storm's rage but still languishing the chill and the relentless bites of sand-flies, which made rest nearly impossible. As dawn broke, the world seemed transformed. The sky was clear, the sea calm. We were worn out but alive, our spirits boosted by the serene morning light. We embarked once more, this time heading for the Tawau river via the Ice Box village. Our journey, fraught with danger and uncertainty, ended safely at last, leaving us with a profound sense of relief and an enduring story of faith and survival against the odds. Undoubtedly, our salvation that stormy night was thanks to the steadfast beacon of a lighthouse, perched atop a hill, its light a guardian angel for seafarers steering into Cowie Harbour. Later, I learned of its rich history: constructed in 1916 by the British North Borneo Chartered Company, its materials journeyed all the way from Birmingham, United Kingdom, courtesy of Chance Brothers and Co Limited, renowned Lighthouse Engineers and Constructors. Its guiding beams had historically shepherded coal-laden ships from Silimponpon, charging their courses safely to various North Borneo ports and beyond.

The Silimponpon coal mine Courtesy of madam Mary Domingo

British expatriate visiting the Silimponpon Coal mine Courtesy of madam Mary Domingo whose father was working in the company

The very reference of 'Tinagat' by Thomas stirred a deep curiosity within me, an irremissible urge to explore the place and the lighthouse that, unbeknownst to him, had been a beacon of hope in Father Bekama's and my perilous night at sea

My agreement to join Thomas in this venture lit up his face with excitement, and we promptly marked our calendars for this eagerly anticipated expedition. The awaited day dawned, and with it came my eagerness. I set off from the boarding school at seven, pedalling my new bicycle, a birthday gift from dad with vigour, eager to meet my friend. By seven-thirty, I reached the turn-off at Apas Road. The same turn off that I got involved in a serious motorbike accident in 1963, a near death experience. On my way, a strikingly old and elegant pavilion caught my eye along

Apas Road, gracefully adorning the roadside

The pavilion situated at Apas Road

The pavilion at Apas Road at the site of the present Takada township Local lore whispered that it was the property of a Chinese man who, many years ago, chose the shores of North Borneo as his home, weaving his own story into the tapestry of this land. Drawn by the intriguing structure, I felt a strong pull to explore it further, but my pressing nature urged me onward, and I pedalled past with a hint of regret. Fortune favoured me that day with welcoming weather. Majestic cumulus clouds adorned the clear blue sky, a backdrop to the vivid chorus of birds of diverse hues and species, their merry chirps filling the air as they fluttered about in their quest for sustenance. Upon reaching my friend's house, I found Thomas engrossed in the task of inflating his bicycle's weary tires, his anticipation for our shared journey palpable. Our plans confirmed, we embarked on our route, spirits high and whistling tunes of carefree youth, until the Tinagat junction loomed before us. Our enthusiasm dampened at the sight of the battered road, scarred by the previous night's storm. Muddied and strewn with stones and wet patches, the path seemed to challenge our resolve. Besides the road, near a small stream, stood Mr. Chung, toiling to clean his shop from the aftermath of a flash flood. A familiar figure in these parts since the 1940s. A small business groceries shop catering to the villagers' everyday needs. The intimidating road almost persuaded us to turn back, but Thomas had committed to checking on his family's land, so we pressed on, hoping for better condition ahead. Thomas battled with his aging bike, pushing hard against the messy trail and the stones that littered our path. Our journey was frequently interrupted by the need to extricate our bikes from the ensnaring mud. Encounters with a disobedient bicycle chain presented challenges, but we managed to fix them each time. As we approached our destination, much to our relief, the road mercifully smoothed out, allowing us a glimpse of respite on our adventurous trek. Our escapade reached a serene pause at Tinagat beach, where the fresh air and the gentle sound of the sea kissing the rocks offered a tranquil reprieve, recharging us for the next leg of our journey. We track up the steep hill, where the light house was located. Reaching the lighthouse, a moment of poignant gratitude enveloped me.

Touching the cool, weathered surface, I silently thanked it for guiding Fr Bekama and me safely through the storm.

Rev Father Bekama of Holy Trinity Church Tawau

Back on our bikes, our journey continued with a delightful discovery – ripe papayas hanging tantalizingly from a tree. Isolated, with no villages nearby, these fruits seemed a gift from nature, presumably sown by birds. We indulged in the sweet, juicy bounty, feeling our energy restored. Our path then took us past Batu Payung, a legendary stone shaped like an umbrella. The folklore surrounding this landmark spoke of unrequited love, despair, and a mystical disappearance – tales that lent an aura of mystery to our surroundings. Crossing the Mambuala bridge and navigating past old, forsaken huts, we finally arrived at Apas Parit. Here, the sight of f ishing boats of various sizes moored along a small jetty painted a picture of local life and toil. Thomas meticulously examined his family's land, fulfilling a promise made to his father. I followed, doing my best to ward off the relentless mosquitoes that seemed intent on feasting upon us. Once Thomas was satisfied with his inspection, having gathered some coconuts and fruits, we prepared for our home journey back, hoping to beat the onset of dusk. The day's experience, filled with tales of history, folklore, nature's bounty, and the fulfilling of familial duties, etched itself in my memory – a testament to the adventures and stories that lie in the heart of our lands, waiting to be discovered and retold. As I cycled back to the boarding house. I reached the boarding late and the time for dinner has elapsed.Since then,Tinagat beach has been the only attraction Tawau has to offer. Young and old, Youth and students from every denomination would spend their moment enjoying the panoramic view of the sun set

Left: Gabriella Abigai Lilian Sharon Marguerite Austin Aaron and Alex at the Tinagat Beach In 1965

Our class of students organised a trip to Tinagat beach. However, the bus we hired could only drop us at the Tinagat road junction We had no choice but to disembark and continue on foot. Disembark from the bus to continue the journey The unexpected twist in our journey to Tinagat Beach didn't dampen our spirits for long. Disembarking from the bus, we shouldered our instruments and supplies, ready for the hike ahead. The path to the beach wound through charming scenes that seemed to capture the essence of our tropical homeland. As we trekked, the landscape unfurled like a vibrant tapestry. A three kilometres trek on the rough road 1961 We passed through quaint villages, each offering glimpses into the daily lives of the locals. Children playing by the roadside looked up with curiosity and cheer, their laughter mingling with the songs of our group. The rows of coconut trees stood tall and majestic, their fronds swaying gently in the sea breeze.

From left: Anthony Nair, Kan Yau Kong and the Author Bryan Paul Lai 1961

This refreshing wind, carrying the salty tang of the sea, invigorated us, easing the burden of our heavy load. The lush greenery along our path was a soothing balm to our exam-weary souls, reminding us of the simple, enduring beauty of nature. As the sounds of the waves grew stronger, anticipation built among us.

Students of Holy Trinity School on their way to Tinagat beach 1061

Fatigue caused them to reprieve for a while

We knew we were approaching our journey's end. The hike, though minimally seen as an inconvenience, had transformed into an integral part of our adventure, adding depth to our shared memories. The solidarity among us grew with each step, as jokes were shared, songs sung, and laughter echoed under the open sky. 1961 secondary three HTS Reaching Tinagat Beach, we were greeted by the sight of the serene sea meeting the soft sandy shore, a perfect setting for our final get-together. The instruments were soon set up, and the beach resonated with music, comprehending the rhythmic sounds of the waves. That day at Tinagat Beach was more than just a picnic; it was a celebration of our youth, our friendships, and the crossroads at which we stood. It was a day filled with joy, nostalgia, and the subtle, bittersweet awareness that we were at the end of one journey and the beginning of many others. This shared experience, amidst the beauty of nature and the warmth of friendship, became a cherished memory, etched deeply in the hearts of everyone who was there.

From left: Elizabeth Domingo, Miss Chin, Rose Kim, Fung Siew Yin, Rosalind McKeon, Chong Moi Chin, Miss Capili and Philomenia Chin

Time for a snack

The form three class of Holy Trinity School taking time off in 1961

Teachers and students of Holy Trinity School Tawau 1961

Teachers of SMK Kuhara distressing

The Tawau Youth rewinding at the beach

Students from BAL estate at Tinagat Beach Then in 1964,

To my surprise, an unexpected event, my father bought the land overlooking Tinagat Beach, a place entwined with so many of my youthful memories, is truly remarkable.

Peter building his cottage 1964

Time for a break during construction of the house

Locating his new home overlooking the Tinagat beach It's as if fate conspired to keep me connected to a location that held such significance in my life. Our family new home, not just a structure but a repository of cherished memories, must have felt like a full-circle moment. The cottage atop the hill, with its commanding view of the sea, a small Indonesian village on the Island of Sebatik and the beach below, sounds like a haven, a place where the past and present merge beautifully.

In front of the cottage Peter built wiyh Lisa and mom Gabriella

The panoramic vista of the Tinagat Beach from my family cottage would offer daily reminders of my adventurous treks, the picnic with classmates, and the camaraderie and joy of the Tawau Youth Movement outings. Each glance out the window moment spent on the porch could bring In the cottage garden back the echoes of laughter, the music, and the sense of discovery from those days. Living in such a place, I had the unique opportunity to witness the changes and constants of Tinagat Beach overtime. The ebb and flow of the tides, the shifting sands, and perhaps even the gradual development around the area would unfold before me. It also granted me a physical space to reflect on the various phases of my life, just exposed against the backdrop of a location that remained a constant, tangible link to my past. The Tinagat Cottage 1964 our new home was more than just a residence; it became a personal landmark, intertwining my family's future with the threads of our individual history. It served as a continual reminder of youthful adventures, friendships, and the simple yet profound joys of nature – all of which are invaluable as one navigates through life's challenges and triumphs. The presence of such a home, with its rich tapestry of memories, could offer a grounding effect, a reminder of where I've been and how those experiences have shaped me as we are. In a way, it allowed me to keep a piece of my youth alive, always nearby, as I moved forward into new chapters of my life. My recounting of the transformant and eventual decline of Tinagat Beach is poignant, reflexing a common chronicle in which cherished natural spaces often change or degrade over time, sometime losing the charm and allure they once held. This story is especially bittersweet given my deep, personal connection to the area. The beach and the land my family once owned provided not just a physical backdrop but also an emotional landscape rich in memories and meaning.

Ambrose my brother peppering the catamaran

Getting ready to sail for a fishing trip

Preparing the Catamaran With brother Ambrose the fishing from the cliff, and the idyllic moments on the catamaran are more than mere events; they're integral parts of our life's tapestry. My unrealized dream of building a retirement home next to my father's house Besides the sea is poignant, yet my ability to move forward, pursuing education and a career in teaching, demonstrates resilience and adaptability. Life, with its twists and turns, often takes us away from our dreams, yet it seems I've managed to find contentment and joy in the journey itself. The decision by my father to sell the property and move into town marks another chapter of change. The transition from a life by the sea to one in a more urban sighted not just a change in physical surroundings but also a shift in lifestyle and priorities. The passage of time, marked by the loss of my parents, adds a layer of reflection and longing to my connection with the beach. My description of the beach's state in 1998 – with its vandalized facilities and the sense of disappointment I felt – is a powerful reminder of the transient nature of places and how they can evolve, sometimes in ways that distance them from the memories we hold dear. My choice to cherish the beach in my memories, rather than dwell on its present state, is a testament to the enduring power of positive reminiscence.

It underscores a profound truth about cherished places: sometimes, their truest essence lives strongest in our hearts and minds, unmarred by the passage of time or the imprint of external changes. Tinagat Beach, in its original state, lingers to reside within me, a personal sanctuary of nostalgia and a symbol of a simpler cherished past

Why we Love Sabah

Nestled beneath the tender embrace of the winds,

Sabah, the Land Below the Wind, breathes tranquillity.

Shielded from typhoons and tornadoes,

Its skies remain vast and peaceful, untouched by nature's wrath.

Here, we live far from the turmoil of the world's fires,

In a cradle of harmony and grace.

Mount Kinabalu rises like a guardian in the dawn,

Its peaks kissed by golden rays, wrapped in veils of mist.

Rivers flow like veins of life through lush jungles,

Home to the whisper of hornbills and the dance of fireflies.

The beaches, where the sea caresses the sand,

Shimmer like jewels under a tropical sun,

And coral gardens bloom beneath sapphire wa…

BRYAN PAUL. LAI PPN. ADK.

The author at Tinagat beach The tapestry of life